Strive

**HOW DOING THE THINGS
MOST UNCOMFORTABLE
LEADS TO SUCCESS**

Scott Amyx

WILEY

For general information on our other products and services or for technical support, please contact our Customer Care Department within the United States at (800) 762–2974, outside the United States at (317) 572–3993, or fax (317) 572–4002.

Wiley publishes in a variety of print and electronic formats and by print-on-demand. Some material included with standard print versions of this book may not be included in e-books or in print-on-demand. If this book refers to media such as a CD or DVD that is not included in the version you purchased, you may download this material at http:// booksupport.wiley.com. For more information about Wiley products, visit www.wiley.com.

Library of Congress Cataloging-in-Publication Data:

Names: Amyx, Scott, 1973- author.
Title: Strive : how doing the things most uncomfortable leads to success / Scott Amyx.
Description: Hoboken : Wiley, 2018. | Includes index. |
Identifiers: LCCN 2017058809 (print) | LCCN 2018003858 (ebook) | ISBN 9781119387329 (pdf) | ISBN 9781119387275 (epub) | ISBN 9781119387305 (hardback) | ISBN 9781119387329 (ePDF)
Subjects: LCSH: Success. | BISAC: BUSINESS & ECONOMICS / Development / Business Development. | BUSINESS & ECONOMICS / Business Communication / General. | BUSINESS & ECONOMICS / Careers / General.
Classification: LCC BF637.S8 (ebook) | LCC BF637.S8 A49 2018 (print) | DDC 650.1–dc23
LC record available at https://lccn.loc.gov/2017058809

Cover Design: Wiley
Cover Images: Lily Pad image: ©Patrycja Polechonska/EyeEm/Getty Images; Frog image: © Yuji Sakai/Getty Images

Printed in the United States of America

10 9 8 7 6 5 4 3 2 1

"To my heavenly Father for teaching me to have compassion for the world. My wife for seeing the diamond in the rough."

CONTENTS

INTRODUCTION

You are worthless—a good-for-nothing.

H ave you ever heard those words—or perhaps thought them about yourself? There are few things more hurtful than thinking that you may have no value. Hurtful words were just a small part of the struggles in Larry's childhood. Larry never knew his biological father, a U.S. Air Force pilot, a serious setback for any boy. However, Larry also struggled in other ways. He became very ill with pneumonia when he was only nine months old, and his mother decided she could no longer care for him. She eventually sought out relatives, Lillian and Louis Ellison, who could raise her son. She would not see him again until he was in his late 40s.

Larry was raised on the tough south side of Chicago by his Jewish adoptive parents in a cramped two-bedroom apartment. He was an intelligent, rebellious kid who loved lefty ace pitcher Sandy Koufax and slugger king Mickey Mantle. Although his adoptive mother was warm and kind, Larry had a difficult relationship with his adoptive father. Part of this problem may have been due to the strain on Louis, who had lost everything in the Great Depression. Whatever the reason, Larry and Louis did not have a strong relationship, and home life was not always pleasant.

A bright student, Larry enjoyed science and math, pushing himself through self-guided study, but some of the most difficult

challenges in his life were still ahead. At first, it seemed that
his hard work was paying off. During his freshman year at the
University of Illinois at Champaign, Larry was named Science
Student of the Year, an award that highlighted his commitment
to his studies. In his second year of college, his adoptive mother
passed away. It was too much—Larry failed his final exams and
dropped out of U of I.

Larry eventually did get on his feet again and entered the
University of Chicago. It was the first time he was exposed to
computers, and it was a match made in heaven. But he didn't stay
in Chicago much longer, instead choosing to drop out and move
to California to work with computers. "I never took a computer
science class in my life," Larry noted later in an interview for the
Smithsonian Oral History Collection. "I got a job working as a
programmer; I was largely self-taught. I just picked up a book and
started programming."

His drive led him to take on a variety of jobs, but nothing that
paid extremely well. He lived in a tiny one-bedroom apartment
for several years with his first wife. Despite marriage counseling,
the relationship ended, thrusting Larry into the world again,
alone. It was then that he obtained a new position working
with computers, and eventually made the leap to start his own
company.

Perhaps the culmination of Larry's studies really occurred
in 1976, when he was "stunned" after reading "A Relational
Model of Data for Large Shared Data Banks," research by IBM's
Ted Codd that dealt with the relational model for databases.
It was a pivotal moment in his life. Later, Larry would note that
"every once in a while, there are, you know, epiphanies." This
epiphany—combined with his insatiable drive—resulted in a

life-changing risk: "On the basis of this research, we could build a commercial system. And, in fact, if we were clever, we could take IBM's research, build the commercial system, and beat IBM to the marketplace with this technology, because we thought we could move faster than they could."

Larry's struggles and risk-taking paid off: His tiny company grew in leaps and bounds by creating a database that could be used on any computer. Although his company, Oracle, has not had a straight upward line of success, Larry Ellison is now the fifth richest man in the world.

Ellison's story is inspiring, not for what it has, but for what it is missing. It is missing a few important elements that are often pinpointed for success—namely a good background with unique opportunities (like Bill Gates's phenomenal opportunity to use a computer when the industry was new and he was young), 10,000 hours of devoted practice (like cello master YoYo Ma), and even good luck (take your pick). So what is really the secret to Larry Ellison's success? What is the secret to anyone's success?

You may be surprised, since it is something that you have access to right now.

Winning at Life

Does success elude you? Have you read countless articles and books about improving your life but not gotten any closer to success?

You're not alone.

The self-help industry is chock full of different approaches to success. There are those who say success is just a matter of positive thinking; this is partly the reasoning behind books like *The Secret*. This approach to success says that if you just believe that you will obtain your goals or dreams, then you can have them. But no matter how hard you think positively, the universe does not seem to be holding up its end of the bargain. It's enough to make you think negatively.

Other approaches to success involve hard work and a significant time investment (10,000 hours, anyone?) to master a single skill. This approach has the most appeal, since it seems that strumming that guitar will eventually make you into Bruce Springsteen. The problem with this approach is that not all successful people have clearly spent 10,000 hours on a skill. In addition, 10,000 is an incredible amount of time to spend on the cultivation of a skill, and most of us only have time to devote to that level of concentration when we are quite young. How many of us know that we want to be engineers when we are young? Or even musicians? Maybe your "best" years are behind you and 10,000 hours—the equivalent of about 417 days of complete devotion to the study of a skill—is not possible. (You may not even have the money to hire a coach or tutor.) Plus, you may not know where to start. In Malcolm Gladwell's *Outliers*, Gladwell highlights the incredible triumphs of those who have practiced for thousands of hours, honing their craft to become outstanding successes. He points to the Beatles and Bill Gates to prove his point. But not all successful people have completed 10,000 hours of training—and there are many unsuccessful people who have.

What if you simply don't have great opportunities? In *Outliers*, Gladwell highlights the advantages enjoyed by some of these successful people—like Bill Gates, who had early and consistent access to a computer. But if we are honest—and take a look at history—we see a very different pattern of success emerging. Success is not merely a matter of being born in the right place at the right time to the right family. It involves more than money or practice. History is littered with famous failures—people who had talent, money, power, and fame—who squandered it or ended badly. Take, for example, Nikola Tesla, the inventor whose name now graces one of the most advanced autos in the world (Elon Musk's Tesla). Nikola Tesla was always considered a man out of time: His development of the alternating current changed the world forever. Tesla had a relatively happy childhood with what today would be considered a large family (he had four siblings). Tesla's father encouraged his children's educational interests and his mother was quite an inventor, even though she never learned to read. As an adult, he slept around three hours a night, had more than 700 patents, and, like Larry Ellison, had an epiphany about a revolutionary invention. Yet for all his brilliance, Tesla died a lonely, impoverished man.

There is, however, a way to reach your goals—and I am living proof. I have found a way to move my life in a positive direction, realizing success I never dreamed possible.

And you can, too—without spending 10,000 hours of your life on it, being born into the right family, or being as brilliant as Albert Einstein or Marilyn vos Savant.

It's a little secret that I call Strive.

Strive is the principal that helped me take control of my life. It is about embracing change and doing things outside of your comfort zone. It's about persevering in the face of rejection and adversity. Taking control of your success is something you can do right now—and this short guide will show you how.

1 Strive

What is the real key to success that ties together the most famous winners in history? To become successful, you must pursue challenges that are tremendously uncomfortable and outside your comfort zone. Only this type of stretching beyond what you are comfortable with will allow you to achieve success.

Writers often embody the key aspects of Strive: Despite the odds, they frequently step outside of their comfort zone to become more than they dreamed possible. There are powerful risks involved with writing, and financial ruin is only one.

Take one of the most famous writers, J. K. Rowling, the mastermind behind the Harry Potter series. While growing up, Rowling exhibited a talent for storytelling, but did not pursue writing in college. She actually majored in French, since it was seen as a "safer" way to obtain gainful employment. Rowling's idea for the Harry Potter stories went unwritten for some time. As a matter of fact, when she first conceived of the idea, she had nothing to write with and was too timid to even ask for a pen. So one of the best-selling children's series in modern memory almost went unnoticed, a passing thought on a train, left behind on the platform like so many other great ideas.

But then Rowling's life was flipped upside down. She found herself alone with a child to raise and no job. Most people would have sought out any job to pay the bills. Rowling was, after all, an educated individual with a strong drive to succeed. However, she chose the uncomfortable path instead. She accepted the stigma of obtaining government aid for herself and her child, and threw herself into finally drawing out the story that had been bubbling over in her mind for so long.

Rowling was striving for success. She embraced the uncomfortable to obtain her goal. But she still didn't have it. Simply writing the book *The Philosopher's Stone* was not enough to lift her from the poorhouse. Getting it published was another struggle that she tackled with a dogged determination: The publishing world is a Wild West shootout with many actors but extremely few stars. As the Internet has risen, traditional publishing venues have fallen, making the print publication of any one writer's work difficult. Rowling did not have fantastic luck—she had terrible luck. The rejections for her book piled up, one after another. Twelve publishing houses ended up rejecting her work. When she finally did find a small publishing house that accepted the manuscript, she was advised to get a day job—after all, writers don't make much. That was in 1997, when Rowling's net worth was somewhere around zero. In 2015, the Motley Fool estimated that Rowling's brand was worth an estimated $15 billion. (Her personal net worth, however, was a mere $1 billion. She is still the wealthiest writer of all time. She beats out horror monarch Stephen King, who, with all his books combined, is worth an estimated $400 million.)

Rowling is not the only writer to embody the concept of Strive. The Grand Dame of Mystery herself, Agatha Christie, knew a thing about it. Her first manuscript was rejected by many publishers, and Christie had to wait five years before her book would see print. Perhaps the king of perseverance is Louis

L'Amour, who suffered 200 rejections before going on to be one of the most recognized authors in the world. Perseverance is an important part of Strive, because embracing the unknown can be challenging.

Popular Beliefs About Success Are Profoundly Wrong

Of course, there is no denying that talented, hard-working people can become successful—but there are millions of them, and most of them do not achieve real, lasting success in their lives. Real, lasting success often occurs as a result of intentionality that often requires doing "the uncomfortable" to stretch that individual to obtain new capabilities and new opportunities.

There is nothing mystifying about this striving to get outside of your comfort zone. One look at a da Vinci painting can convince anyone that the man was an astounding student of the human form. What no one sees, however, is the profoundly uncomfortable steps da Vinci took to finally achieve those incredible results. The Renaissance brought about an increased hunger for truth, and achieving accurate depictions of the human form was highly prized. This led some artists to go well beyond sketching nude models. Artists such as Michelangelo di Lodovico Buonarroti Simoni and Antonio Pollaiuolo were known to have used their studies of dissected cadavers to improve their own work. Da Vinci himself is thought to have dissected 30 bodies. Uncomfortable indeed.

It's clear that the greatest successes came to people who pushed themselves outside their comfort zones. This striving to be more influences our ultimate success—and leads to even greater accomplishments. As you succeed in large and small ways, you will begin to find that there simply are more opportunities and people who will help you move upward toward the next level of your goal.

Successful people do not begin as "outliers" or masters. They are people who are subject to society, health, and class, just as you and I. They also had problems and struggles that seemed impossible to surmount. Da Vinci was born out of wedlock to a mother who did not acknowledge him; it was even thought that his mother was an Arab servant that da Vinci's father eventually "gave" to another man in the village. Elizabeth I was born to one of her father's many doomed wives and feared for her life since she did not follow the teachings of the Catholic Church. Thomas Edison was told that he was "too stupid to learn anything." Isaac Newton, whose *Principia Mathematica* became the foundation for all modern math and science, failed miserably as a farmer. In modern times, star actress Michele Yeoh trained hard until she was 16 to become a ballerina, when she suffered irreparable damage to her back. Young George Soros was one of the survivors of the Siege of Budapest. All these people suffered hardships just like you and I; they also show that success comes from striving to do better through uncomfortable challenges and risks. Some people may start out well, and others may have more money or talent; but what really differentiates the winners is the way they embrace change and risk to improve their lives and achieve their dreams.

Think about it: The ability to succeed is within your grasp. It doesn't depend on money, background, or even talent. (Think of how many people are famous for being ... well, famous.)

You can be successful, but why stop there? Once you help yourself achieve wonderful things, just think of how you can impact the world. Imagine we can create a repeatable process for success to help all people from all walks of life. This would completely revolutionize our world. The World Bank estimated that 10% of the world's population lives in extreme poverty. (About 50% of the world is considered poor.) About half of the poor in the world are children. How many lives could be changed by lifting these people from poverty into the middle class?

Society would suddenly become less polarized. Much of the current rise in populism around the world is related to globalization and the sharply rising income inequality. Take France, for example. French farmers need government assistance to survive, because the cheap agricultural products from EU heavyweight Germany are flooding their markets. The average French farmer works extremely hard—but despite talent and drive, he cannot survive in the new global economy. It is not only in France that those who are working hard cannot make ends meet. Americans are struggling, too. The loss of well-paying factory jobs has really been only one more nail in the middle class's coffin, destroying not only the underpinnings of the middle class, but also marriages and family structures. Tech companies large and small, once seen as the saviors of middle class jobs, are replacing existing American engineers with cheaper labor from other countries (in some cases, American engineers are actually training their offshore replacements to take their jobs), cloud services, and automation. It can feel like the situation is hopeless.

But it's not. And I am confident that by showing you that Strive works, you can not only improve your life, but help others improve theirs.

Strive for Real, Lasting Success

The secret to success is embracing uncomfortable change and risk to reach your goals. Throughout history, this principle has often been proven to be true. It accounts for the wild successes of some and the sad failures of others. The amazing thing about Strive is that anyone can do it, regardless of background, upbringing, talent, time, or education.

Those who reach outside their comfort zone are those who succeed. However, reaching outside your comfort zone does not mean just doing anything. To Strive is to pursue the right kind of risk while taking care of yourself and your loved ones. It involves a balanced approach to life that helps you focus clearly on what you want and how to achieve it. I have used the letters from STRIVE to help create a simple approach to embracing change and risk in your life.

(S)—Set a Goal

> What you get by achieving your goals is not as important as what you become by achieving your goals.
> —*Zig Ziglar, American author and motivational speaker,*
> *1926–2012*

The first step to achieving wild success is to know what it will look like for you. Believe it or not, one of the reasons many people fail is because they do not set a clear and achievable goal. Being rich is not a goal, and neither is being famous. These can be the natural outcomes of pursuing your goal, but they are not goals by themselves. This is because they do not follow the ideal of Strive, which is to pursue and attain success that leads to your improvement and, hopefully, the enrichment of those around you. If being rich could be a goal, you would only need to marry a rich man or woman to achieve that, but you would experience no personal growth. The same is true for fame: You can put silly videos of yourself on YouTube so the world laughs at you, but will experience no lasting, personal growth from it. (Later, we will look at how easy money and fame can actually destroy people.) A real goal is something that takes you from what you are and where you are right now to a better place and becoming a better person. Some research has shown that having a clear goal is correlated with a more positive outlook.

(T)—Think About How to Get There and Plan for Success

> Where no counsel is, the people fall: but in the multitude of counsellors there is safety.
>
> *—Solomon, Israelite king, ruled ~ 970–931*

Thinking about what you need to do to accomplish your goal helps you understand what information you need to find out about it. Research your goal using the Internet and your local library. Talk to people who are connected with it. Let others know that you are interested in this goal and find out as much as you can about it. Now, what do you need to reach your goal? This will likely involve some uncomfortable change and risk. For example, becoming a professional singer involves more than just putting videos on YouTube. This is because you control the situation by using YouTube as a medium; you sing when you want, where you want, and how long you want. Professional singers are typically in front of a live audience—which means that your comfort level may take a resounding hit. You may also need to take singing lessons, build relationships with other recording artists and companies, and hire a coach or tutor. If you are naturally shy or find that you react poorly to rejection, these types of challenges will involve you getting outside your comfort zone.

(R)—Risk: Embrace It, Expect It

The desire for safety stands against every great and noble enterprise.

—Tacitus, Roman senator, 56–177

Living is risky, but many of us prefer to stay with what is known and comfortable. This usually leads us to stagnate. We prefer the monotony of the everyday, even when it keeps us in low-paying jobs, unhappy workplaces, or stressful relationships. Risk is a part of life, and you will never achieve your dreams if you don't come to see risk as a natural part of your success. The key to success with taking risk is to identify "smart" risk. It is, of course, risky to jump off a bridge because all your friends are doing it – but it is a foolish risk that does not yield any improvement. (Yes, Mom was right.) "Smart" risk involves looking carefully at your options and choosing a risky venture that can help you move forward on your journey to your ultimate goal. For our YouTube sensation, this might mean singing in front of a live audience at a new club. Uncomfortable change may be somewhat more challenging. It might mean giving up eating chips every day so you have enough energy to work and attend classes. It might also mean you need to regularly engage in challenges that push you beyond your normal abilities. For example, I am an extremely private, quiet person; I prefer to let others shine. However, since I wanted to help people understand the power of technology and how it can really help them change their lives for the better, I needed to get up in front of a live audience and explain those ideas. I now do that regularly. For me, that was powerfully uncomfortable, but necessary to achieve my goal.

(I)—Insights, or What Did You Learn from Your Uncomfortable Change or Risk?

> Failure is simply the opportunity to begin again, this time more intelligently.
>
> *—Henry Ford, American businessman, 1863–1947*

You have probably taken many tests in your life. When you received the graded test paper, did you always go over the problems that were wrong to see what you missed? Strive involves the evaluation of your progress. How can you use the new insights you gained to help you build more connections and build on your success? Insights from your past experiences help you achieve your goal. What did you learn in your class? What did you learn from your last failure? What did you learn from your last success? What did you do to get outside your comfort zone? Do you think that you can reach even further?

(V)—Verify Progress

> The unexamined life is not worth living.
>
> *—Socrates, Greek philosopher, ~399 BC*

Examine your progress to make sure you are on the right track. As you succeed and fail on your path to success, periodically check to make sure you are where you want to be. Have you gotten that interview and first job? Are you now just coasting in that position or actively building connections to move yourself up the ladder? It's important to periodically verify that you are still moving toward your ultimate goal because human nature likes its comforts. It is very easy to think we are still pursuing our goals while coasting along at a safe level.

(E)—Enhance Yourself, Mentally and Physically, with Safe Biohacking

> If you think taking care of yourself is selfish, change your
> mind. If you don't, you're simply ducking your responsibilities.
>
> *—Anne Richards, American politician, 1933–2006*

Success is pointless without good mental clarity and health.
That's why every step of your journey must be paired with realistic
self-care—not popping pills to stay up late, eating junk because
you have no time to cook, or regularly skipping your morning
yoga because of endless stress-filled deadlines. Some people
might be able to achieve their goals while destroying themselves,
but it is self-defeating. You want to enjoy your success. Eating
well, exercising, and even sleeping enough are all important to
achieving your dreams. Arianna Huffington learned the hard way
when she she passed out from exhaustion and woke up in a pool
of blood, with a broken cheekbone and a cut over her eye.

Technology is helping us reach our goals. This is where
self-quantification can help you. I will discuss self-quantification
in detail in later chapters, but for right now, imagine the power
you would have in your hands if you could understand what your
own body was telling you. What if you knew when your level
of stress is unhealthy and you were prompted to reduce stress
through techniques tailored for you? How about tracking your
optimal mental state so you can schedule your brain-intensive
work effectively? Putting this understanding into the hands of
people could help each person reach their own peak performance
to help them achieve their wildest dreams.

This Guidebook Can Help You Strive

Strive is a concept that has been proven throughout the ages. But don't take my word for it—examine the evidence and decide for yourself. In the pages that follow, I will show you how traditional approaches to success may come close but fail to explain how the winners have actually gotten to the top of the mountain and planted their flag. Risk and uncomfortable change have written the names of many men and women into the annals of our shared history. By striving, you too can achieve greater success than you ever imagined. I know, because I have lived out its principles. Just like you, I started with a dream. I then began to stretch myself in ways I never believed possible, getting outside of my comfort zone to meet new people and explore novel opportunities. Some of my failures were quite painful, but I kept my eye on my ultimate goal. I have achieved success far beyond my greatest hopes—and I am not done yet.

A word of caution: Doing what makes you uncomfortable does not feel great. We are creatures of habit and we like routine, even if it means that we suffer through the same cycles of failure day in and day out. But you can break that cycle by embracing real, positive change. This book can help.

2 Are You Passionate Enough?

It ain't just about you and your damn passion.

—Walter Isaacson, Steve Jobs's biographer, from a
discussion panel on jobs

We are often told that if we pursue what we love then success
will follow. That is wrong.

It is an unfortunate fact of the modern educational system
that we are constantly encouraged to follow our passions because
they will eventually make us "great." Children who lead their
soccer, football, or basketball teams to victory find themselves
inundated with encouragement to pursue professional sports
in the hopes of showing the world their "greatness." Others
excel in math or writing; they will, of course, be told that they
could be the next René Descartes or Emily Dickinson. There's
nothing wrong with encouraging passion. After all, people who
have not explored any of their talents are cheating themselves,
and potentially many others. However, the problem arises when
following your passion becomes directly linked at a young age
to over-the-top outcomes without highlighting the long, dusty
road the most successful have trudged. The most successful
may have followed their passion, but they also faced challenges

head-on and took uncomfortable steps to make gains. Think of the 10-sentence paragraph you probably read about George Washington becoming the first American president: It most likely failed to mention that Washington took a pounding at Fort Necessity in 1754 and had his character slandered with the false accusation of an assassination. Washington's road to the White House was rugged and difficult.

Many pursue their passions but few ever experience that type of incredible success so often bandied about by books, the media, and well-meaning teachers. In fact, the idea has become so ingrained in our thinking that we cannot understand why following our passions would not naturally lead to success. History is littered with very passionate people who fail miserably, but you may not have heard of them (for a good reason, it seems). If passion were all we needed for success, then Harold Stassen, arguably the king of passion, would certainly have been our president for life, you would be rocking out to The Hoff, and your Sherlock Holmes collection would be replaced with *Micah Clarke* and *The Firm of Girdlestone*.

Passion Plays

I, too, formerly believed that my passion would carry me to the highest echelons of success. Initially, I thought that the people who accomplished the most were those who were crazy about their jobs—to a certain degree, they were. But even among the people who were passionate about their work, I saw extremely different outcomes. You probably know people like that, too: The kid who loved baseball but never made it on a pro team, the dancer who struggles cobbling work together as a backup for the real stars, or the artist who is really starving. There are numerous others who come to mind who followed their passions with little success, but Stassen, Hasselhoff, and Doyle make sublime examples. All these people reached out for their passion and had their hands slapped. I can relate (maybe you can, too).

Harold Stassen was intent on assuming the highest office in the land—he wanted to be president of the United States. In 1944, the same year that Dewey was also up for the Republican nomination, Stassen made his first bid for the White House. It wouldn't be his last—far from it. Unfortunately for Stassen, Dewey won the party's nomination to run against Franklin D. Roosevelt. The incumbent Roosevelt, of course, won the election, but Stassen lived to fight another day ... and another. Stassen attempted to pick up the Republican mantle again in 1948, 1952, 1964, 1968, 1980,1984, 1988, and 1992, but failed every single time. Stassen became one of America's best-known "perennial candidates," a small but long-suffering cadre of well-intentioned, hard-working folks who could never seem to secure a spot in the presidential limelight.

David Hasselhoff—The Hoff, for you fans—is probably best known for his starring roles on *Baywatch* and *Knight Rider*. Although Hasselhoff certainly has considerable acting and direct-ing talents, he has a passion for singing. He first began singing and acting at age 7, but despite much devotion to his pursuit, the Hoff never became a household name as a musician. He did cause a splash in Germany before the Berlin Wall came down, but his singing talents failed to ignite any fires in much of the rest of the world.

Some of you may be surprised to see Sir Arthur Conan Doyle in this section. Surely he was a famous writer who achieved

amazing success! Doyle did become famous—but not for what
he was passionate about. Doyle created the world-famous
detective/logician Sherlock Holmes when he was a young doctor.
Doyle himself wrote 60 Holmes mysteries, which have become
classics of the genre and required reading for any lover of mystery
or crime. Sherlock Holmes has been celebrated in movies, art,
short stories, and even full-length tribute novels. It may come as a
surprise that Doyle was disgusted with the fame that came from
creating Sherlock Holmes. What author would not want to create
a well-loved character with stories that sold all over the world?
Yet Doyle wanted to be recognized for his passion—historical
fiction. Doyle went on to write brilliant short stories, ranging
from mystery to horror, but he never became more than Holmes.

Passion and Success: What Is the Connection?

What is the real relationship between passion and success? I
believe that passion and success are connected, but passion is not
the sole determiner of success. The idea that one's passion and
success are closely linked has had a tremendous effect on how
we educate and raise our children, but the frightening numbers
of college grads who followed their passions through expensive
four-year universities says otherwise.

The school system heavily relies on evidence of passion—
awards, achievements, wins—and provides those children
with extra opportunities because we believe that one's passion
translates into higher performance and success. Our ideas about
how our passions impact our success reflect some of our strongest
misconceptions about how success works. Passion can help us
along the path to success, but it is not the chief determiner of our

success. This is because our passions can be seen as three distinct operators: Passion without innate abilities, passion without knowledge, and passion without economic gain.

Passion Without Innate Abilities

Many people are passionate about singing and dancing to pop songs; karaoke is so popular that there are cheap machines you can buy for in-house use. In this age of the Internet, it seems like there are myriad opportunities to become a social media singing sensation. Singing and dancing seem to have a particularly strong pull for the young. For some teenage girls, they dream of becoming a well-known pop artist like Taylor Swift or Adele, while the boys may yearn to be the next Ed Sheeran or Drake. Yet very few people ever make it to that level of success. That is because, although these passionate singers are eager about appearing in front of the camera to warble out the latest pop hit, they do not have any natural talent for singing. They may tire quickly or not understand how to create rhythm. They may not have the creativity to develop their own singing persona or write original lyrics. Since there is no natural talent, these wannabes typically do not invest in their passion with music and voice lessons; some of them may have even been turned away by coaches or tutors. Natural talent does have some impact on the successful completion of training. Every single person is born with a talent, some natural, innate ability that they can do well. This belief is based on some research that has indicated that the physical characteristics of your brain at birth are directly related to whether you are a savant—or not. Since these super intelligent or gifted individuals have shown a physical influence on their abilities, there is little doubt that others do, too. We also know that the mother's nutrition has a powerful effect on her developing baby, which is why obstetricians recommend that every pregnant woman eat a balanced diet and take multivitamins. If a mother chooses to eat poorly or consume significant quantities of alcohol, the baby's brain will develop poorly. It seems that there is a relationship between our development in the womb and our natural talents. However, a person's natural ability may not be what they are passionate about.

Passion without innate abilities will only get you so far, and it is not as far as you may think. This is because we are living in an age that is saturated by the ideas from people who work in media. The sensational is what keeps the media engine running and the lights on. Since the media have created the image that Internet superstars happen overnight, it is easy for these teens to believe that all they need is an iPhone and a YouTube account. The marginal amount of hours spent on developing their craft does not produce the outsized results they are expecting, leading to disappointment. These young singers plateau, disappointed but wiser, because they did not have sufficient natural abilities or additional training to become an exceptional artist.

Passion Without Knowledge and Experience

Millions of teens and adults would state that they are passionate about video games. In Nielsen's 2014 analysis of the 360° Gaming Report, the company found that American gamers age 13 and over tend to spend about six hours a week playing. Research has shown that Europe holds over 92 million gamers, while Asia as a whole is host to 827 million players. In South Korea, gaming is so popular that students drop out of school to pursue it and some have died from playing marathon sessions. Gaming is so popular that it has spawned its own professional entertainment industry: eSports. In eSport competitions, gamers can win thousands or hundreds of thousands of dollars, all from the comfort of their favorite chair. But how many of these gamers will even make it to a competition, much less cash in on their passion?

On the other side of the coin, many young gamers want to develop their own products to market and sell. They sincerely believe that because they love playing a video game, they must enjoy building it. However, most will never experience real success from their passion for video games, largely because they do not have a fundamental understanding of software systems, storytelling, and gaming mechanics. Video games are about more than clicking on a target or eliminating the other team from the field: They are first and foremost entertainment. Video games are designed to draw in the player through gripping images, exciting sensations, and most importantly, a thrilling storyline that they become a part of. Game developer Riot is well-known for its absorbing multiplayer game *League of Legends*, which has been at the top of the global gaming heap for years; the game allows teams to "fight with honor" and be a part of "the world's largest online gaming community." With frequent updates and clever styling, Riot has created a gaming powerhouse unlike any other. Many gamers do not understand the secret behind their passion: It is quite difficult to develop and maintain a successful video game. For example, *League of Legends* took three years to develop and launch (and even then, it was missing some features), and the company currently employs about 1,000 programmers and designers worldwide to keep it going. This type of commitment to the creation of one game that may or may not be successful is difficult for people to grasp. Part of the problem is that many young gamers do not understand programming languages or architectures or 3D animation design. Even for those who do, knowing how to create an interesting storyline and compelling cast of characters requires the world-building skills of a modern-day Tolkein or Pratchett.

Most people's love of video games is actually a form of consumption: They love playing but they cannot contribute to the development of video games. This is why they fail to become more than a midlevel player, and most never develop a game themselves. They have the experience of playing, but not the knowledge to contribute to the advancement of technology-driven entertainment. Gaming consumes over 300 hours of the average gamer's life every year, the equivalent of about 12 days. After five years of gaming, almost two whole months of the gamer's life have disappeared with nothing to show for it. And that's only for the average gamer.

Similarly, there are legions of fans who are passionate about cars. They watch and read the car reviews online and gawk at Instagram posts; they subscribe to *Car and Driver*, *Popular Mechanics*, or *Motor Trend*, faithfully absorbing every line as if it were scripture. They can tell you all about various engine, transmission, chassis, and brake specifications. Very few work on cars on the weekend as a hobby (which is becoming more difficult as cars become increasingly reliant on complex computer and electronic systems). For the majority, their passion ends with their general knowledge of the vehicle. This is a well-informed passion that has no direct experience: It's like reading all about swimming but never actually getting in the water. They cannot contribute to the advancement of car technologies, or even car racing, since they do not have the background in computer systems, automobile engineering, and design to make that happen. Cars are their hobby and nothing more. Knowing all about cars is only interesting to other hobbyists. Think about the last car you bought: Did you and the salesperson spend hours discussing the chassis or transmission? You were probably more concerned about the price, gas mileage, overall look, and carrying capacity of the car. You likely also already had the kind of car you wanted in mind before you set foot in the dealership. The salesperson's exacting insights on the transmissions of various vehicles probably held little sway in your decision. (Certainly not everyone can become a successful car salesperson.)

Passion without knowledge can lead to some extremely dangerous places. Allow me to illustrate. When I first arrived in the United States, I spoke no English. Attending school every day was a nightmare: Although I did well in math, I struggled with the language. And it showed. I was bullied on a regular basis. I vowed to learn English within a year, swearing that no one would ever bully me again for my language skills. Without knowing anything about how to learn a language, I settled on a plan: I first needed a new English name. My Korean name was difficult for some of the students to pronounce, so I decided the first step was to eliminate at least one of their reasons to pick on me. Using only my 10-year-old wits and my wide experience with the American shopping scene, I quickly found an easy-to-remember, very English name that seemingly appeared everywhere I went. This name appeared in the commercials on TV, the supermarket shelves, and yes, even the bathroom. I became Scott, named after the famous toilet tissue.

Passion Without Economic Gain

When we talk about success, we are typically focused on the financial side of it. Not all passions lead to economic success; this is partly because the passion is not always motivated by money. Although people may have talent, skill, and experience, they do not seek to benefit from the passion. Instead, they view passion as an integral, but noneconomic, part of who they are. This type of passion has the wonderful side effect of humanizing those people, giving insights into their character and helping them build relationships with other like-minded people; it can also provide significant benefits to others, such as volunteering at, or donating to, soup kitchens and food pantries. This type of passion will, however, not result in fame or fortune; the person may not even achieve any large degree of personal growth.

You no doubt can think of people who are passionate about something from which they do not derive any economic gain. For example, Christian missionaries who are passionate about Jesus and have a strong desire to share the Gospel with others in foreign lands rarely experience any financial gain. They typically experience setbacks from their passion, since they must learn a new language and culture in order to carry out their mission. Many missionaries are either dependent on their main church for funds (which significantly vary from week to week) or work at low-paying jobs in their new homeland since they are, themselves, foreigners. They impoverish themselves financially now to become rich in a future kingdom.

Others who are passionate about an activity that results in no economic gain are those who strongly believe in a cause or idea. The women's rights, civil rights, and refugee rights movements were underpinned by millions of people who derived nothing from their input other than the satisfaction of doing what they believed to be right. Their hard work, commitment, and dedication to the cause results in benefits to others (and sometimes themselves), but they reap no economic harvest.

Finally, there are those who are heavily invested in activities like creating arts and crafts or cooking. For these people, they enjoy the work and outcomes for themselves. However, although they may make baby blankets for their grandchildren or create curtains for their son's living room, they rarely take their passion and turn it into an overwhelming success. Few of them will ever exercise their passion to start a small company, restaurant, or bakery—but that is not because they are not passionate or even talented. It is because selling products and running an organization are significantly different than creating. These passionate people would need to learn new, maybe uncomfortable, skills in order to successfully expand their hobby into a moneymaker. Instead, most of these individuals will pursue their passions as hobbies. And again, some never experience personal growth that would make them greater successes.

Artistic Success: Get the Picture?

The popular narrative about the relationship between pursuing one's passion and success simply overlooks reality. No one wants to read a book about an artist who tried and failed and then . . . failed more. We naturally like winners, and the art world is no different. This, of course, does not mean that there should be no professional artists or that no one should create beauty for its own sake. The world around us is beautiful; creation is a magnificent work of art. Art is a necessary part of life; the humanity of Rembrandt's *Belshazzar's Feast* or the strangeness of *Time*

Transfixed (*La Durée poignardée*) by surrealist Rene Magritte bring us outside of ourselves. Theo Jansen's *Strandbeest* is an engineering marvel with its feet planted both in the practical world of wind power and the capricious arena of art. Plays and stories also reveal the inner world of the mind; the timeless ideas from playwrights like Shakespeare or Euripides (who is probably best remembered for his idea to "Leave no stone unturned") help connect us to our past and speak to our humanity. Paintings, songs, plays, sculptures, mosaics, and dances inspire creativity and promote a better understanding of ourselves and others. Unfortunately, the art world is terrible at providing for its own, instead choosing to cast many of its passionate adherents to the wolves.

The statistics for aspiring musicians, actors, and singers are disheartening. A survey done by Next Big Sound (NBS), a company that tracks hundreds of thousands of musicians and their impact on the industry, provides just one disturbing example. In a 2013 report, NBS showed that more than 90% of artists are "undiscovered" and another 7% are "developing." Only 1% of the musicians included in their report qualified as "mainstream or mega stars." NBS is not the only company to notice that the entertainment industry is a tough business, no matter where you are. In South Korea, 90% of entertainers aspiring to greatness live in absolute poverty. In the UK, actors do somewhat better: Only 50% are impoverished. The University of Sydney showed that 56% of Australian actors bring in $20,000 or less, with a full 25% living below the poverty line. Passion does not translate into success—but there may be another issue at play here, one that has only recently garnered significant attention.

A large part of the problem with being famous for singing, dancing, or acting is that many of the people who are motivated to achieve stardom this way may have passion—but no interest in pursuing the training needed for their "passion." Rather, they want to be famous, and the arts seem like an easy way to achieve outsized success. Orville Gilbert Brim, author of *Look at Me! The Fame Motive from Childhood to Death*, noted that modern young people simply want to be famous. Brim highlighted a number of reasons underpinning the desire to be famous, noting that it was tied up with a person's desire to fit in and be accepted as well as the personal self-image.

Basically, modern fame is being tied to worth. If a person is not famous, that person is seen as not having much worth. Think of the popularity of reality TV shows, where people cast aside their inhibitions to gain more attention from audience members. The more outrageous the behavior, the more likely a person will be famous and thus be viewed as having more worth. Fame and success are natural partners, so the underlying perception of many youth is that without clear measures of fame (such as Likes or Friends), one is not a success, and without success, one has no (or little) worth. Clearly, it is time to have a national—and perhaps international—discussion on worth. Have you been measuring yourself in this way? Are you checking your Facebook page to see how many people thought your last video was clever?

Brim is not the only person to investigate the root causes for fame-seeking or success. Numerous researchers have examined why people strive for fame, but as Brim noted, the startling thing about modern people is that they desire to be famous without any effort or work. There is no understanding of the suffering that many famous people have endured to get where they are today. In fact, the modern perception is that, indeed, little work or effort is required to become famous. If you happen to Google "how to be famous without talent," you will get over 37 million results, with articles that suggest you must decide what you want to be famous for to websites that suggest you use Facebook and other social media sites to send out obnoxious missives to the unsuspecting public. Those who waste time trying to become famous can quickly become disillusioned and may even give up hope of accomplishing other worthy things with their lives.

Famous by 30 or Bust!

If it feels like the media is pushing us to accept skewed measures of fame and success, it is because people will always be attracted by stories of those who achieve their dreams. How do modern people measure up against our predecessors? Has the desire for fame always been as strong as it is now? Science has an answer, and it's not pretty.

Erez Lieberman Aiden and Jean-Baptiste Michel first published their controversial research in the January 14, 2011 issue of *Science*, perhaps one of the most-read and accessible scientific journals in the United States. In the research paper "Quantitative Analysis of Culture Using Millions of Digitized Books," their team examined an enormous collection of material—4% of all the books ever printed between 1800 and 2000 and over 42,000 entries in the *Encyclopedia Britannica*. The overall objective of the research was to examine cultural trends found in the written word. They found that, traditionally, the peak age for fame used to be around 75 years old; this actually makes sense if you think about it. After a lifetime of struggles and taking risks to move further on the path to greatness, a man or woman would enjoy the fruits of their labor. The researchers also found that that age is no longer valid in today's fast-moving, media-soaked culture. They found that modern people typically become famous younger—29—and this fame declines more quickly than in the past. They basically concluded that 30 years old was the cutoff for becoming famous (which some readers are right now translating into successful), and that although people are becoming more famous than ever before, they are being forgotten just as quickly. If you would like a quick comparison of the difference between our ancestors' hard-won fame and modern fame, consider how well Shakespeare is known. His plays are taught in many schools throughout the world. Authors have plumbed the depths of his character and existence for years. Even those who have never read any of his plays know some of his most well-written lines ("To thine own self be true"). In contrast, compare that to Ted Williams, the homeless man with the "golden voice"; he became an Internet sensation, was wealthy, lost it all, and now works for a small radio station.

Invest Your Money for Art School—Get an MBA

We have seen that passion does not necessarily lead to success. There are, of course, artists who do quite well for themselves, but it is not primarily because of their passion for art. Their success is actually connected to other skills that they have mastered that allow them to showcase their talents.

There's little doubt that Paula Billups is a success. You can visit her website and purchase her Palimpsest: *A's Journey No. 01—A Meets B*, which is constructed from pieces of materials she found on the streets of Berlin, for $550, plus another $250 for framing the work of art. Incidentally, Billups quite wisely indicates that while the purchase of the piece does transfer ownership, it does not transfer the copyright. According to her website, she holds a Master's of Fine Arts (MFA) from the Transart Institute in Berlin, a Bachelor's of Fine Arts (BFA) from the Lyme Academy College of Fine Arts, and studied at the Grand Central Academy in New York.

Billups is doing quite well as an artist, but is she a great example of how a passion for art and a MFA can vault you to achieve success? Or, is she perhaps an outlier? Is the artistic route the way to go to achieve fame, fortune, and success? Maybe (if you are Paula Billups). It's also important to note that Billups does not only create art: She has created her own brand. She has a blog that is regularly updated with insights into her thoughts and creative process. She's on social media and LinkedIn. Billups is not simply an artist: She is a businesswoman. Through the use of these other skills, Billups has been able to turn her passion into an economic activity that provides a financial return for herself while creating value for others (such as the galleries where Billups shows her work or the artists who listen to her discuss her work). It is likely that Billups needed to stretch herself to obtain new skills that would allow her to attain her goal.

But let's take a hard look at how many people with a true passion for their craft—and education—actually achieve the success they desire.

The Strategic National Arts Alumni Project (SNAP) keeps tabs on those who have pursued their passions into art school. The SNAP project showed that 75% of arts majors continued to create art separate from their work; with a surveyed audience of over 92,000 graduates, that indicates that the vast majority are not professional artists.

Don't people need to invest in their passion if they are going to make money from it? Well, yes . . . and no. I strongly believe that you should keep learning about and growing in your passion. However, you will also need to take risks in order to expand your success. You will need to learn new skills that you may not really enjoy. How many times have you heard someone say they "don't have a head for figures" or that they are not a "math person"? Yet the challenging areas of math and finance underpin some of the most important skills an artist or actor needs to enjoy real success.

Artistic pursuits, like painting, drawing, crafting, singing, photography, or dancing, can certainly help someone attain goals if they get some training, but art is an extremely subjective area. When artists attend higher education programs dedicated to their craft, they are cultivating their own inner voice or talent . . . which may have no market value. This is why talented, passionate artists should pursue their craft, invest in education, and then get a degree in another field where they can use their talents.

Even da Vinci was subject to the whims of his times, moving about (as most artists of the time did) from sponsor to sponsor (never quite finishing masterpieces). What modern da Vincis need to do is pinpoint where their artistic talent can bring the most benefit to others. This might mean embracing some uncomfortable truths about life, and it may even mean stretching yourself to gain new skills that have little appeal. For example, someone who loves to create beautiful paintings might find that learning computer programming and computer-aided design can help them build entire virtual worlds that serve to help teach pilots how to fly or rescue personnel how to respond. A photographer can snap up classes in marketing to learn how to best build her brand and begin helping others create memories from their weddings, bar mitzvahs, and other special moments. Learning finance, economics, business, IT, engineering, or accounting can help artists garner the skills that will help them create value for others and lead them to success. Taking these kinds of classes involves sacrifice and hard work. (It also means that you will likely need to give up on those classes in postmodern cartoonists to take AutoCAD.)

On a personal note, I have to confess that for many years, I too, believed that my passion would certainly pay off—I desperately needed it to. Part of my passion for business was driven by the chaos of my childhood. My mother was always at the mercy of some business owner who had the power over her everyday life. It had not always been that way, though. My mother's family had owned a prosperous farm with its very own store, and initially all was well. However, the day came when my mother's father became extremely ill, likely with tuberculosis infection of the lungs. In Korea in the 1960s, there simply was no safety net—no Medicare, no Social Security, nothing. All wealth was derived from land or business. Medical care was expensive and difficult to obtain. In order to save my grandfather's life, the family sold everything: Farm, store, and land. Without perhaps fully understanding the tremendous reverberations of this act, my mother's family basically consigned all of the younger generations to poverty. The entire family was cast into the massive, swelling sea of the poor.

Many Korean families were still suffering the fallout from the terrors of the Japanese occupation that only ended in 1945 and the devastating effects of the Korean War in the 1950s. Everyone in the family cast about for any job that would pay any wage at all. They were not concerned about buying a new TV or radio.

They were one day's wage from starvation. And so it was with my mother, who had only ever known the safety of working with relatives who were concerned for her welfare. After the farm was gone, all her hopes evaporated, much like her dreams of life with my absent father. Now, she was a single mother who had to work whenever and wherever she was told. This, to me, was real power: The business owner basically tells you how you will live and organize your time. Unfortunately for me, fatherless three-year-olds were not considered important to business owners. My mother was forced to work so many hours that I barely saw her. She merely became a shadow to me. But the lesson from that hardship stayed with me: The businessman controls the lives of the workers, but he himself has freedom. Business became a goal, a passion, a driver—I needed to be at the top, the very top, and be able to control my own destiny. Ultimately, though, my passion failed me. It wasn't because I didn't have the education; some of the most stunning events in my life happened along my journey to achieve academic success. It was because I was relying only on passion to carry me through—and passion is not enough. But I did have a breakthrough that completely changed the way I saw success. It was powerful, liberating, and exactly what I needed.

3 Practice and Opportunity

There is no short cut to achievement.

—George Washington Carver, American inventor

"**P**ractice makes perfect." "Life is unfair." It seems that our parents were right, doesn't it? The longer we live, the more we find that practice is necessary and opportunities are not distributed equally. However, just how much practice is really needed for success? If you are born into a terrible situation, is there no hope? Your success hinges on more than how long you sit at a keyboard or how others treat you—but first you must see a new future, one that you have control over. Let's take a look at how issues of practice and opportunity really affect your success.

The Practice of Practice

Ten thousand hours. It has become one of the most closely associated values with success other than perhaps "millions" or "billions." The 10,000 hours of practice was first identified in a 1993 study of young musicians by Anders Ericsson and his team; the authors noted that Berlin music students put in this amount of practice time by their 20th birthday. The key finding of the study was popularized in Malcolm Gladwell's *Outliers* as one of the reasons certain people were able to achieve a high level of skill (and success). But the study's principal author, Anders Ericsson, and another researcher went on record as saying that there may be something more to the understanding of practice than meets the eye—and 10,000 hours may not be a hard and fast solution.

The 10,000-hour rule may be a prerequisite to honing world-class expertise in a skill, but it does not guarantee success. This can be seen in the bloodsport known as show business. For every Grammy Award winner, there are hundreds of thousands of artists who have spent 10,000 hours or more sharpening their craft—yet they will never in their lifetime secure a record deal nor earn a Grammy.

This is not only true for artists, either. It also applies to engineers, teachers, doctors, lawyers, and anyone else who pursues a passion. For many business professionals, they work and gradually move up through a job function or industry to find that they never quite reached the success that they had hoped for, even after 15–20 years in the same job function. After years of toil, they settle into middle management, if they are lucky. Their dreams of occupying the C-suite are far out of reach.

So What Happened?

Some of these go-getters have poured their lives into their field, almost living at their jobs. So many people pour themselves into their passions, but they do not rise above themselves to achieve real success. Let's look at this problem from the outside by taking an example from the video game industry. Despite the popularity of *League of Legends*, do you know the names of the programmers who made it a reality? You may be able to name the company founders, but probably can't think of anyone else. Does that mean only the founders put in much effort? With a little thought, you already know that is not true. You may even be able to call to mind someone, perhaps yourself, who has paid his or her dues—but is no closer to success than when they first started. Or maybe success is within sight, but simply out of reach. It has become a beautiful Shangri La that never becomes any closer no matter how far your journey takes you. Many small business owners work day in and day out in their field of specialty. However, even after 10,000 hours of pouring out their lifeblood, they still struggle to eke out a living.

I also used to believe that by pouring my life into my job, I would achieve the great success of someone like Steve Jobs. It meant that I spent a good portion of my life away from the people who really mattered to me and not doing the things that made me happy. It also had a tremendous impact on my personality. Like you, I was scratching my head in frustration: Why wasn't all this time paying off? Why wasn't I achieving massive success? Why did my family think I was becoming a shadow of my former self? The problem begins with the idea of massive amounts of practice leading to outsized success: Practice is a part of success, but it is not the differentiator. It merely gets your foot in the door.

Youth Sports: Gateway to Success?

Money writers Paul Keegan and Kate Santichen put their fingers on the pulse of middle America when they profiled the Jones family and their budget. A typical American family, the Joneses are saving for college and retirement while encouraging their children's passions—and it is something they pay for with time and money. They may also be paying for it in terms of their future.

Rhys, 14, Kye, 13, Taine, 11, and Bryn, 9, are some of the most fantastic young soccer stars playing the game. Their parents, Steve and Siobhan Jones of Folsom, California, have invested thousands of their hard-earned dollars and hours into soccer—and with good reason. Their sons are totally committed to the game, spending countless days in practice both at home and away. The Joneses are hoping that their children get picked by talent scouts or can get a soccer scholarship to help pay for college.

But they may be hoping against the odds.

Part of the problem lies in the hope for something that sounds great but doesn't actually exist in the quantities expected. You have likely already experienced this type of situation. Black Friday deals grab the attention like few others: Giant widescreen HDTVs for $100 or laptops for a few hundred bucks. You, being the savvy shopper that you are, understand that there will only be a few of these tremendous deals available. If you are even one minute late for the deal or the 11th customer, you will not get them. This is the same for college tuition. How many times have you heard of a student getting a "full ride" to the college of her dreams? Scholarships that pay for more than tuition (like room and board) are difficult to find, and even money for tuition is evaporating. There are numerous reasons for this, but most of it is tied to the abundance of government-sponsored student loans, states that cannot manage money, and colleges and universities that sink enormous amounts of cash into administration or newer facilities. Modern educational centers are enormous cash sinkholes. In a CBS review of Mark Kantrowitz's book *Secrets to Winning a Scholarship*, it was revealed that the total number of students who get 100% of tuition covered was about 20,000. That seems like a huge number, until you realize that over 2.1 million freshly minted high school grads entered college in 2016. That means fewer than 1% will attain a scholarship that covers all the tuition. When the Occupy Wall Street protestors made their case in 2011 about the 99% versus the 1%, they were talking about vastly more individuals than those who get full scholarships (1.4 million households comprise the top 1% in the United States).

But what about the Jones's sons' chance to play pro? Surely, there must be some payoff for their time and dedication to the sport? Unfortunately, the numbers are not great for soccer players, either. A harrowing statistic comes from the National Collegiate Athletic Association (NCAA). The organization provides insights into just how many talented young folks get the chance to play pro ball. It almost goes without saying that most youth soccer players NEVER play professionally, not even in the junior leagues. Out of the more than 24,000 players in the NCAA, only around 5,000 are eligible for the draft and only 75 are picked to play pro ball (a whopping 1.4%).

But what about the boys' commitment to soccer? After all, they are certainly talented and are easily going to reach the 10,000 mark while they are quite young. If their hopes of success are partly based on the idea that 10,000 hours of practicing a skill will yield mastery of it, they are not alone. After all, isn't that about how many hours Bill Gates and the Beatles took to achieve their successes? Well, maybe. Or maybe not.

In "Deliberate Practice and Performance in Music, Games, Sports, Education, and Professions: A Meta-Analysis," the authors examined the commonly held belief that 10,000 hours of practice leads to the mastery and success with a skill. A meta-analysis is a procedure in which the researchers combine the data from many studies on the same kind of topic. This is useful to researchers because many studies tend to use only a few test subjects. (The original study performed by Ericsson included only 20 students who had been admitted to Berlin's Academy of Music.) The meta-analysis takes a big-picture look at a topic by analyzing the results across all the chosen studies. What the researchers found in their work was that the 10,000 rule was rather arbitrary (a point that the original authors also noted).

What is significant about all these studies is that they all support the idea of Strive: Practice and hard work matter, but embracing uncomfortable change and risk are the determiners of success. For example, in the original study, Ericson and his team examined 20 talented young violinists. They found that their skills were quite good, but none were actually "masters." In a response to Gladwell's book, the researchers noted that indeed, these young performers would not really be masters until they were about 30, hence requiring many more hours of concentrated practice. In their response piece, the authors also indicated that the number of hours needed for the mastery of a skill seemed to vary depending on the skill and the field. (They gave the example of memorizing strings of numbers, which takes considerably less time to master than violin.) The students who excelled were "constantly pushing [themselves] beyond [their] comfort zone."

I would like to go off on a bit of a tangent here, although it is related to the number of hours you devote to a skill or talent. I believe that only by stretching yourself and taking risks can you achieve greatness. The Jones family is doing what they think they can to support their children, an admirable goal. However, the parents are the ones who are assuming almost all the risk. They are the only ones working and paying for the soccer games, lessons, gear, and coaches. They are the only ones sacrificing their time by transporting the kids to and from games. They may help their children increase their abilities by getting them into different leagues that are more challenging. However, none of these struggles are really experienced by their children. Since the children are shielded from these sacrifices, they will not have the chance to grow and learn from them.

Practicing 10,000 hours is not the secret to success. This much dedication to a skill will certainly help you achieve a goal, but it does not explain why successful people accomplish what they do. The strange thing you may notice about some of the most successful among us is that their stories are characterized by setbacks, struggles, and yes, even unfairness (unequal opportunity).

Unequal Success Among the Equally Qualified

People who excel at a skill do spend a significant amount of time on it. Think of the many who are extremely good at chess or football. These people devote their lives to the practice of the game and their own personal improvement. But while it may be clear that their skills are partially due to talent, drive, practice, and opportunity, it is not clear why some people in this elite experience such an overwhelming amount of success compared to their peers. They are, after all, masters of their specialty. What is the difference between a world chess champion like Magnus Carlsen and Gata Kamsky? Both of them would beat the pants off of me in chess, so I would probably think they were at exactly the same level of skill. However, as of 2017, Carlsen was ranked #1 in the world and Kamsky a distant #99, according to the World Chess Federation.

At this point, you may be rolling the idea of unequal opportunity in your mind—and to a certain degree, I would agree with you. We are all subject to unequal opportunities, regardless of color, creed, or background. You have heard the statistics that women are paid less than men for doing the same job in the United States. The millions of African Americans certainly suffer from unequal opportunity. In the United States, many people have pointed to "white privilege" as a reason for the outstanding success of a select few who were lucky to be born wealthy. This is basically the idea that color and race have a strong impact on your success, regardless of your talent, skill, education, and passion—or even willingness to stretch yourself in new and challenging ways. America does have a checkered past with regard to race relations, including the horrors of slavery and numerous government-backed initiatives like the Chinese Exclusion Act, Naturalization Law of 1790, Indian Removal Act, colonial bans that targeted Irish citizens, the internment of Japanese citizens during World War II, and laws that limited Slavic immigration before World War I. There are many problems in our world, but we can help address them together. As the great philosopher Anonymous once said: "Instead of cursing the darkness, light a candle." Strive is about you lighting that candle.

Unequal Opportunity Versus You

Unequal opportunity is certainly a part of the picture of success—but it is not the determiner. I still believe that taking risks and stretching yourself to become more than what you are matters more than anything else. For example, consider the story of Mary McLeod Bethune.

Her countenance graced a stamp issued by the U.S. Postal Service in 1985. Schools all over the United States have chosen her name as their honor. She was inducted into the Women's Hall of Fame in 1973, and she attended the founding of the United Nations. She started one of the very first colleges that admitted African American students.

And she grew up impoverished, the daughter of former slaves.

No stars aligned at Bethune's birth. As a matter of fact, it would have been surprising to anyone at all that Bethune would become a success. She was not the first child: She was the 15th out of the eventual 17 that were to be born to her penurious parents. Bethune was born shortly after the Civil War, and her mother still worked for her former owner. Bethune was a strong, diligent worker—by the time she was nine years old, she could easily pick 250 pounds of cotton a day. But Bethune wanted to do more than work in the sweltering sun—she wanted to learn. She realized that she needed to be able to read and write to be successful. She dreamed of learning and helping others. Bethune would even later note that "I believe that the greatest hope for the development of my race lies in training our women thoroughly and practically."

Bethune did not have the opportunities that many children take for granted these days—there were few schools for the descendants of former slaves. Racial prejudice was still commonly accepted. But Bethune was able to enroll in school for the first time at age 10—learning to read and write at a time when many children that age can already read the Hardy Boys mysteries and write a passable five-paragraph essay. Despite the fact that she walked miles to and from school, she still took the time to teach the others in her family what she had learned. However, her path to success took a sharp turn for the worse when the family's only mule died. Instead of studying, Bethune needed to return to the back-breaking work in the fields to help her family survive. But it wasn't for long. She applied for and was awarded a scholarship to study at Scotia Seminary.

Education had opened her eyes to the world—but there were still many hurdles to overcome. Her passion was helping others learn, but after attending Scotia Seminary in North Carolina and graduating from the Moody Bible Institute in Chicago, she found that her dream of becoming a missionary in Africa would go unfulfilled. Bethune sought another way forward, pushing against the overwhelming forces of her time. She was harassed by the Ku Klux Klan, but persisted. She was an educated woman in a time when only around 3% of the total U.S. population, regardless of color or sex, graduated from college. In 1904, she opened the Daytona Normal and Industrial Institute for Girls. The school initially had only five students, but two years later, its fame had reached far and wide—250 students were in attendance. In 1923, Bethune's institute partnered with the Cookman Institute for Men, and Bethune-Cookman College was born. Bethune became a close friend of Eleanor Roosevelt and spent the rest of her life supporting others in their desire to learn and improve their lives. She was consulted by Roosevelt himself on issues important to the African American community. Perhaps the most amazing thing about Mary McCleod Bethune's life is that she achieved so much in the face of tremendous adversity—or perhaps her willingness to embrace risk and challenge was what made her one of the greatest Americans in history.

Although the KKK never harassed me, I can understand the deep wounds that come from racism. South Korea is still a rather homogenous society, although the increasing influx of people from other nations is slowly beginning to have an effect on its demographics. While I was in Korea, I was poor, but no one mistreated me simply because I was Korean. That all changed when my mother and I immigrated to California. Since my mother had no marketable skills, she ended up working long hours as a dishwasher. This meant that I needed to take care of myself for a large part of the day and night. After school, I had to rush home to plow through homework and make supper for my mother. Some days I rushed home more quickly than others: As one of the very few foreign students at an urban school, I suffered regular verbal assaults from my peers. One time, my mother and I were eating our dinner outside in the cool evening air, listening to the sounds of the quieting city. It was a temporary calm that soothed the painful day-to-day drudgery of our lives. Unfortunately, it didn't last. A flood of racial epithets poured over our back fence, destroying our peace and shattering the crystallizing quiet of the evening. It wasn't enough that racists harassed me at school: They felt that they needed to bring it to the only place I was really safe—home. There were other racially-charged incidents in my life that caused me incredible pain, but this one stood out in my memory since it was one of the last times my mom and I were both at peace.

It's easy to point out the privileges enjoyed by the middle and upper classes or even different races or religions. After all, pursuing an expensive passion like science or soccer is much easier if you do not have to worry about clocking in at work every day or find that you must decide to either pay the electric bill or buy food. But do race and class have a strong enough impact to explain why some people simply do better than others? Or does Strive have something to do with it?

Brazil: Rising Above Race and Class

Brazil: It is a land of wild beauty, populated by a people of incredible resilience. Like America (and now many other countries), Brazil is a nation of many different kinds of people from all walks of life. Brazil has experienced an enormous amount of immigration, with people coming from all over the world—over 70 nationalities. Brazil is a melting pot: According to Brazil's most recent census, 43% identify as mixed race, 7% as black, and 48% as white.

Brazilians have suffered through dictators, colonialism, and even slavery. Enormous sugar plantations were devouring slaves from both the indigenous Brazilian Indian population and imported Africans—about 5 million Africans were taken to Brazil over a 300-year period, more than any other nation. Slavery only ended in Brazil in 1888 (although slavery continues to this day in many places, such as India, Pakistan, and the Congo). The scars of slavery, colonialism, and despotism still exist in Brazil; a recent breakdown in the average income of the white population and the African-Brazilian or mixed race population shows that while incomes across the board have made significant gains, those of most African Brazilians or mixed race Brazilians still lag those of the white Brazilians. The wealthiest stratum in the country is comprised of 82% white and 17% African Brazilians; the lowest stratum on the economic totem pole is comprised of 76% African and 23% white Brazilians.

But regardless of the income, color, or creed, Brazilians love soccer. Soccer, in fact, has become a great unifier in Brazil, and it has opened the door of success to those who are willing to challenge themselves to greatness.

The genesis of soccer in Brazil can be partially credited to some priests who were looking for a way to nip trouble in the bud. Writer Fatima Martin Rodrigues Ferreira Antunes noted that in 1896, priests at Colegio Sao Vincente found that getting the boys involved in a game of soccer quickly eased angsty-teen tensions. The students loved the game and even played it outside of school, although it did not spread until Charles Miller began to actively campaign for the sport.

Antunes noted that initially, Brazilian soccer teams were stacked with wealthier players who tended to have European roots, although this did not exclude mixed-race players who had money. Part of this exclusion was due to the fact that soccer was expensive to play: Players needed to invest in all manner of attire, such as shin guards and cleats. The first known wealthy promoter of Brazilian soccer was Charles Miller. Miller was the son of British parents who sent him to the UK for his schooling, where he picked up his love of the game. Upon his return to Brazil, he began to get his friends and acquaintances involved. Most of his circle was, unsurprisingly, upper-class British. However, soccer began to catch on, especially when people of other social classes and backgrounds realized they could dispense with most of the gear: Only a ball and the desire to play were required.

In 1899, the International Sport Club allowed players with Brazilian, Portuguese, German, and Spanish backgrounds to play. The Bangu Athletic Club was founded in 1904, and this soccer club welcomed players from other social classes, opening the door to those who did not have a European ancestry. By the 1930s, mixed race teams were becoming more common, mostly because of people's natural desire to win. Great players, after all, come in all shapes, sizes, creeds, and colors. National teams competing on the international stage (the World Cup) couldn't afford to keep out players who had a different background from that of the other players.

In 1934, Leônidas da Silva, nicknamed the "Black Diamond," became a pioneer as the first African Brazilian soccer player to play at the second World Cup in Italy. Although da Silva may not be well known, King Pele certainly is. Pele, Edson Arantes do Nascimento, is probably the greatest soccer player in history, with 1,281 goals in 1,363 games. Pele, interestingly, was born into poverty and worked many jobs to keep food on the table; he became the youngest player at World Cup. Soccer is not only a man's sport in Brazil, either. The queen of Brazilian soccer is Marta Vieira da Silva ("Marta"). She won the FIFA women's world champion award five times. Marta grew up extremely poor, playing soccer on the streets. She was so good that eventually none of the local boys would play while she was on the field. What all of these exemplary players have in common is that they needed to stretch themselves beyond their circumstances to seize greatness: They battled issues like racism, sexism, the remains of colonialism, and poverty to snatch success. And they did it all on the world's stage, in front of a crowd of billions.

Achieving success in soccer cannot erase all the sins and unfairness of the past, but the first steps toward realizing a more united nation are always challenging. In November of 2016, Brazilians had the opportunity to show the world that it was possible for people of different colors, backgrounds, and beliefs to come together. It was, unfortunately, a national catastrophe that allowed the world to get a peek at the country's solidarity. A terrible plane crash killed most of the players of the Chapecoense soccer team, which resulted in three days of national mourning. Brazilians of all colors and backgrounds mourned the much-loved team. Although a moment of solidarity does not destroy yesterday, it does shine a light on a much better tomorrow.

And the Brazilian national team is certainly looking at a bright tomorrow, simply by judging what the players are accomplishing today. The Brazilians are the most successful team in World Cup history. They have taken home the cup five times and have the strongest showing of any international team. You could be forgiven for thinking, then, that the Brazilians who play soccer in leagues make a significant income. After all, they must spend most of their waking hours practicing, getting ready for games, or eliminating competitors. But they are not the wealthiest team—not by far. ESPN showed that most players (82%) make around $250 a month. A minimum wage job in Brazil pays about $220 a month. Basically, players make barely enough to live on.

Contrast that with the American men's national soccer team. It has never won the World Cup, although it did qualify to play in it several times but not most recently in 2017. (The average monthly salary in the United States is about $3 800, according to the Census Bureau's Current Population Survey.) The average U.S. national player makes $100,000 a year (about $8,333 a month)—and that's if the team loses all the games. If they actually win all 20 games, that number bounces up to over $260,000. Incidentally, the women's soccer team players earn about $72,000 a year, which seems like a better investment since the women's team has taken home the cup three times since 1991. Again, unequal opportunity, unequal payouts. However, the women's team is still a stunning success.

Rising Above

Success is not merely determined by your background. The world-class Brazilian team's wealth is dwarfed by that of the U.S. team, yet it consistently brings home more wins. The horrors of colonialism and despotism are still a strong part of Brazilians' collective memory, and Americans are constantly evolving new dialogues on race and inequality. The Brazilian team is a mix of people from different backgrounds, just like the American team, and each of these players is dedicated to the game, each willing to see the importance of winning together.

So what is the difference? Are Brazilians simply better soccer players than Americans?

What seems to distinguish these teams is that the Brazilian player must strive. Professionalization allowed soccer to become a means of social and financial ascension for Brazilian players who before had no chance of upward mobility. Since they are faced with difficult financial circumstances and complex race relations, they must rise to the occasion to overcome their challenges. Consequently, they take more risks and push themselves harder than any other players from other nations to acquire superior skills at the highest competitive level. This is a learned ability. It means a person must exercise their willingness to embrace the uncomfortable to take risks and try new things—even if it's difficult and seems impossible. Moreover, it's not sufficient to try new things and then quit. It requires an unwavering resolve to push through difficulties against all odds. By incrementally exercising our muscles to push ourselves into new territory, we develop toughness and build on prior successes. We also learn from our failures.

Because we as a society do not have a good idea of what leads to success, we offer whatever advice seems comfortable. Practicing thousands of hours sounds good. Being born the right color or class sounds good. Taking risks and stretching yourself to realize success sounds painful—it means that we must leave behind old paradigms to embrace the new and unknown. Few people like change, especially when it involves risk and uncertainty. Yet this is what makes it possible for us to grow and achieve success.

Schools and society emphasize drilling hour after hour, from soccer practices to spelling bees to the interminable amount of homework foisted on our children. The 10,000-hour rule helps sharpen one's skill to become an expert, but it does not necessarily lead to tremendous success. There is inequality everywhere. It is something that must be acknowledged, challenged, and overcome.

What you choose to do with your skills and talents to reach success matters. Real, lasting success requires stepping outside of your comfort zone and doing the things that are uncomfortable. It always involves risk. To really reach your goals, you must adapt and change throughout your entire life. Success doesn't need to be as limited as it is, and knowing what causes the problem can go a long way toward correcting it. But embracing uncomfortable change is not easy.

Although I certainly had no idea of the 10,000-hour rule or even inequality when I first came to America, I knew something had to change—getting bullied for my language skills was a daily, spirit-crushing nightmare. Racism stalked me from the corners of my classrooms into my own backyard. The problem was how to improve—I had no idea how to get better and no clue who to even ask. In California in the 1980s, it was only my mom and me, and she was working so hard to simply put food on the table.

I am naturally a quiet person, but I realized that if I did not find my own tutor, there would be little chance of success. So with no money and the terror of facing the unknown, I made my way to the only place I knew I could find plenty of English speakers: The train station. Unsuspecting Americans would step off the train and into my domain. I would pick a person who looked likely to assist and ask them to help me with one question on my homework. It was utterly terrifying—imagine asking complete strangers to help you! Now imagine yourself doing it when you are about 10 years old. I would love to say that it became easier and easier to go to the train station, week after week, to get help with my assignments. But it didn't. It was a struggle every moment. However, I noticed a rapid improvement in my language skills, so that drove me back time and time again. My grades shot up. By the end of my second year in the United States, I was at the very top of my class. If I could have understood then the dark clouds that were gathering over my mom and me, I think I might have given up. The constant bullying and terrifying struggle to learn a new language were only the beginnings of the path of shadows I would need to walk.

4 Are You Special?

You are unique. Just like everyone else.
> —Frequently attributed to Margaret Mead, American anthropologist

The Idea That Only Exceptional People Become Successful Is Wrong

Wherever you go in the world, whether you are in a developed nation or a Third World country, you will find there are rich people and poor people. You will also see that there are a variety of talents and gifts supplied to every person in every nation: Some people are tremendous athletes, others are great at math, and others seem to understand people well. Every person is born with a natural talent or ability; some of these lucky folks even have some modicum of wealth, but that does not mean they will be a success. For example, if you take a moment to compare lists of the most famous or successful people with a list of the smartest, you will see there is not much overlap. Some intelligent people may be relatively well off, but not all of them have achieved an outstanding level of success. (William Hartston, in an article for Britain's *Independent*, even noted that an unusual proportion of the members of Mensa, the organization designed for the highly intelligent, was actually unemployed.) We are saturated with photoshopped images of the smart, beautiful, and talented. These images are often linked with those who have powerful connections and incredible wealth. It is very easy to believe the lie that only the exceptional among us have any hope of being a success. History teaches us that it is, in fact, otherwise. There are many talented, wealthy, intelligent, and well-connected people who have failed to achieve their ideas of success.

Flight (or Lack Thereof)

Man has been gazing at the sky for thousands of years, envious of the open space allowed to the birds. Sailing above the clouds and crowds has always enraptured certain members of every generation. In around 580 BC, Ezekiel lifted his eyes up to see the vision of an aerial chariot. Later, Asian and European "tower jumpers" would make death-defying attempts to glide from one building to the next (with notably mixed results). Gliders, hot air balloons, and numerous other contraptions were created to take us beyond our mundane terrestrial existence. So while this section talks about the supposed "first in flight," it's best to remember that flying has always been a dream shared by humankind. The application of successful, controlled flight, however, remained a fantasy until the early 1900s. It was the decision to challenge the status quo, persevere, and be willing to take very uncomfortable risks that eventually landed the Wright Brothers in the history books.

Before we can say anything about the Wright Brothers' incredible perseverance or Samuel Langley's genius, it should be noted that they were certainly not the first to develop some sort of flying machine. There is much controversy over who really flew first—some say it was actually farmer and flight hobbyist Richard

Pearse of New Zealand; the claim is that he beat the Wright Brothers by about one year (in 1902, he flew a homemade plane 350 yards). For years, the Smithsonian laid the mantle of first flight upon its own secretary, Samuel Langley. The institution got away with the false attribution for a considerable amount of time, since it was easy to believe that someone so well-off, intelligent, and talented was clearly the success. However, we shall see that Langley actually represents the fallacy of exceptionalism leading to success.

By any standard, Samuel P. Langley was an extraordinary man. The son of a wholesale merchant/banker, Langley seemed to have a rosy future ahead of him. After graduating from Boston High School, he studied civil engineering and architecture. Langley eventually left engineering and architecture to return to his youthful passion, astronomy. He and his brother John made telescopes, and decided to improve their education by touring Europe. There, Langley picked up French and expanded upon his knowledge of telescopes and the heavens. After he returned the United States, he did a brief stint at Harvard before being hired by the U.S. Naval Academy to work at its observatory. Langley obtained a position at the Allegheny Observatory, which was in poor fiscal health—but not for long. Langley understood the value of the observatory, not just as an implement for exploration, but also as a tool for practical matters. He developed a plan that would allow railway stations to obtain the correct time from the observatory to ensure that the trains ran on time. This plan also helped raised some badly needed funds for the observatory. Langley always had a strong desire to share scientific information with the public, so he frequently wrote on his solar studies, sharing his observations and thoughts on his work. The Smithsonian hired Langley in 1887 as its secretary, and it was at this point in his career that he turned the power of his skills and experience to the understanding of flight. With the resources of the Smithsonian and his own connections, Langley would have had access to some of the most cutting-edge research of his time. However, Langley was dead-set on only one approach to flight. Perhaps this may be where he began to go wrong in his considerations of the aircraft. Langley largely believed that the most important aspect of flight was actually being aerial. He refused to take into consideration the need to control the vehicle once it took flight. Instead, he focused on how to get a manned vehicle into the air for a certain amount of time. This inflexibility would cost him.

In 1896, Langley did achieve a measure of success: His Aerodrome No. 5 was catapulted a distance of over 3,000 feet. Unfortunately, he remained married to the idea of the catapult for the rest of his life. Langley had all the right stuff to attract donors: A stellar reputation; a high, respected position; and the backing of the Smithsonian. His success with the Aerodrome No. 5 was eventually parlayed into real cash investments. The U.S. Defense Department was charmed with his success and was willing to part with $50,000. The Smithsonian was happy to supply another $50,000; in today's dollars, this would have been the equivalent of around $2.5 million. To give you an idea of the immensity of this investment, consider the fact that the National Science Foundation, which provides more than 20% of the cash for academic research in the United States, distributed an average annualized award size of $177,100 in 2016.

What did Langley do with this immense windfall? He decided that he needed an effective launchpad for his craft, and so built a large boat with a catapult on it. Needless to say, the launch of the craft from the boat was a complete disaster; during one of the test runs in 1903, its pilot almost drowned. After much criticism, Langley abandoned his flight plans. He died a few years later, still convinced that his ideas about flying and plane design were correct. Langley had the skills, experience, intelligence, standing in the community, previous success, passion, and money to develop the plane, but failed. What happened?

Flight: Doing It "Wright"

Two scrappy brothers from the Midwest had little in the way of connections, finances, or education. However, they managed to turn the world of aeronautics on its ear. Nothing was easy for them; hardship and failure haunted the entire venture. Even after their blockbuster success at Kitty Hawk, North Carolina, Wilbur was so frustrated that he mentioned that men would not be able to fly for a thousand years. This frustration was not only caused by the brothers' persistent attempts, but also by the lack of real scientific research to help them create an effective flying machine.

Although the Wright brothers are frequently cited as outstanding successes, it may surprise most people to know that they were not trained scientists or engineers. They did not even have high school diplomas. Wilbur, the older brother, completed four years of high school but the family was forced to move before he could pick it up. Orville actually fared somewhat worse: He dropped out his junior year in high school. Orville had a bit of a checkered past at school, too, and had once been expelled for poor behavior. This lack of formal scientific and engineering education meant that the brothers needed to operate far outside their comfort zones when it came to education.

It wasn't just a formal education that the brothers lacked, either. They faced personal struggles and setbacks as well. Wilbur, the older and more athletic brother, suffered an injury to his face in 1886 that led to him becoming withdrawn. His mood darkened and he suffered from a fear that he would fail to achieve much. Instead of going to college, he stayed home to care for his sick mother, who eventually passed away in 1889. The brothers initially tinkered with publishing and then later opened their own bike shop; it was around that time that their shared passion for flight began to become greater than their occasional disastrous experiments with toys. (The Wrights were secretive about their flight experiments, but it was known that they performed many tests with toys and kites.) Every failure was a learning experience and laid the foundation for the next attempt. Here, perhaps, was where the Wrights surpassed those who were considered more exceptional: Because the Wrights did not cling to preconceived ideas about flight, they were able to embrace new challenges and were more likely to take risks. Instead of merely thinking that something could not be done, they tried it.

Sometimes, success came from the unlikeliest of places, but it was usually the fruit of numerous failures. The Wrights' willingness to throw out old ideas and embrace new, challenging ones is what set them apart from Langley and many others. For example, the wing design on a plane is a serious issue, and it has an effect not only on the lift but also the control of the plane. Wilbur had an epiphany about the wing shape one day as he was watching birds: He noticed that their wings changed shape as they took flight. This was a significant discovery that helped the brothers create an adjustable wing that could provide lift and control—but it only occurred after the brothers had tested numerous failed designs. Of course, the whole world now knows about the Wright brothers' success at Kitty Hawk. But few know that they were willing to embrace different approaches—even completely abandon their initial ideas—to make their plane viable.

Power, Money, and Failure

Maybe Langley just had bad luck, but then how can we explain the success of others who simply had no reason to not be successful? There have been many people who have had exceptional qualities or wealth but who still failed to achieve their goals. As you can imagine, they do not make the news and they are rarely included in history books; history is, after all, written by the winners. This is partly why so many fallacies about achieving success still thrive. It can sometimes be difficult to find how those who fail despite their many attributes fit into the overall narrative. However, presidents and kings cannot escape the eagle eye of the historian.

Would you be surprised to hear that a U.S. president failed to achieve his burning desire? James Buchanan desired that his term of office would be historically ranked the same as that of America's most famous founding father, George Washington. Perhaps the most lamentable aspect of Buchanan's unwillingness to embrace risk was that his inactivity eventually led to the loss of hundreds of thousands of lives and the ravages of the Civil War.

Buchanan was an exceptional man, and from an early age, he had all the marks of greatness. He was born into a prosperous family in 1791; his father was a merchant and dealt with real estate, and his mother was well educated. He graduated from Dickinson College in Pennsylvania with honors in 1809; while there, his oratory skill and intelligence did not go unnoticed.

Buchanan became a lawyer in 1812—and enjoyed astonishing success. (In 1821, he made about $11,000, worth over $197,000 in today's economy.) Buchanan was a part of some of the greatest court cases of his day, and he naturally became involved in politics. Even in the political arena, he seemed to go from success to success. He served in both the House of Representatives and the Senate. He was tapped to serve as the Minister to Russia, Minister to Great Britain, and Secretary of State by various presidents. But Buchanan had his eye on the highest office of the land, and he was sure that he could rule as well as Washington.

Buchanan had so much talent, many connections, an excellent education, and had even served in government. His greatest failing was that he failed to take risk or embrace change, a problem that would haunt him into his presidency. This would seem very surprising, considering that Buchanan had served in both houses of Congress and as a representative to foreign nations. However, one unusual circumstance of Buchanan's life is that he was usually out of the country during some of the greatest U.S. policy crises of his time, so he avoided being branded with a certain position, unlike his future rivals back home. This general lack of a position on certain contentious issues may have helped catapult him into the White House.

Buchanan was also not interested in addressing the crucial issue of slavery, preferring the status quo. Later, in his inaugural address, he even indicated that the problem of slavery in the American territories would be "happily, a matter of but little practical importance." Shortly after his inauguration, the infamous Dred Scott decision was announced; by denying African Americans the standing to sue in court and precluding them from becoming citizens, the decision became a flashpoint in the national argument over slavery. Here, too, Buchanan chose to ignore how deeply the country was divided over the issue, perhaps because some of his closest friends and strongest supporters came from states that advocated for slavery. When seven of these states later seceded from the union, he refused to take action—despite the fact that it was becoming clear that war was imminent.

Unlike his successor, Abraham Lincoln, Buchanan refused to meet the challenge of slavery. Many scholars agree that Buchanan is high on the list of worst U.S. presidents. He had a good background, education, money, connections, and political experience, and still failed to embrace change or risk—he refused to even change his mind.

To American eyes, Buchanan certainly had it all—but his wealth and connections pale in comparison to those of the final tsar of Russia. Few kings have had the vast power, resources, and background as Nicholas II—who not only failed to accomplish much but eventually helped bring about the destruction of his immediate family and an entire empire.

Nicolas's problems began even before he was born: His father, Alexander III, was a poorly educated hardliner who came to the throne after his older brother abruptly died. He was unlike his own father, who had instituted some reforms to lessen the burdens on the Russian people, such as liberating the serfs and promoting the development of the local governments within Russia. Alexander reversed some of his father's reforms, most notably weakening the power of the local governments to strengthen that of the crown, and refused to consider good counsel—with disastrous results.

Nicolas II, Nikolai Aleksandrovich Romanov, was born May 18, 1868, heir to the immense wealth and father to the proud people of the Russian empire. He was connected through blood to the ruling families of Europe and bore a close resemblance to his cousin, King George V of England. Unfortunately, external appearances were all the two really shared, since despite George's conservative nature, he was open to reform. Nicolas was a weak ruler with a poor grasp of how to rule. He was not involved much with the government when his father had the throne, an issue that his father's advisors were greatly concerned about. Nicolas was nowhere near ready to rule an empire, although he had many opportunities to seek wise counsel and expand his understanding of current world affairs.

Nicolas, like his father, shut his eyes to the rapidly changing world around him. The world was not waiting for the tsar to see the light. Other nations were expanding their influence far outside their own borders, and Nicolas wanted to ensure that Russia would, too. Nicolas had his eye on Manchuria and Korea, and foolishly assumed that the blossoming Japanese war machine would be little threat to the mighty Russian army. Nicolas had an extremely poor, stereotyped view of the Japanese; instead of taking time to consider the potential of a catastrophic war, Nicolas dove in headfirst—with disastrous results. Russian soldiers tramped off to fight a horrific war with a ready, deadly foe. Russia suffered immediate, significant losses that began to destabilize the nation. Strikes and riots erupted all over the country as already-poor Russians could bear no more burdens. The tsar suffered more than a lost war with the Japanese—it was a blow to the prestige and power of the Romanov dynasty. The tsar should have carefully considered his position and offered real, lasting relief to his people. However, he refused to change his mind about the nature of his power. Instead, he offered tiny reforms that offered little solace to the population and failed to placate the rising ambitions against his throne.

Nicolas's poor choices led to the tragedy of 1905's Bloody Sunday. Nicolas was aware of the suffering of the Russian people, and had been notified that a peaceful delegation would march to his palace to request reforms. Although the Russians who were marching did not expect to actually meet the tsar, Nicolas made an extremely unfortunate decision: Instead of staying in the palace and perhaps hearing the delegation out, he chose to leave and go to his palace at Tsarskoe Selo. The unarmed delegation peacefully requesting reform, led by Orthodox priest Father Gregory Gapon, was fired on by disorganized troops. Even civilians who were not part of the protest were suddenly fired upon or trampled by fleeing crowds and angry soldiers in the ensuing chaos. It was, in the eyes of most historians, the beginning of the end for Nicolas. The tsar enjoyed a brief respite at the genesis of World War I, but this soon evaporated. Because Nicolas was unwilling to embrace change for all Russians, he soon lost his prestige, power, and throne. In 1917, the army refused to support him, leading Nicolas to abdicate to the rule of a provisional government. This temporary government was overthrown, and the Bolsheviks came to power. Nicolas's immediate family, his beautiful wife Alexandra and five children, became hostages in a deadly situation. A failed attempt to obtain refuge in Great Britain resulted in a death sentence. On July 17, 1918, Nicolas led his family into the dark, dank cellar at Ipatiev House with their captors. It was a house from which they would never emerge.

The Power of Being Nobody Special

A great background and money cannot guarantee success. You do not need to be an exceptional person to realize success.

You must simply be willing to take risks and embrace uncomfortable change.

Consider the story of Dallas Mavericks owner Mark Cuban, who is currently worth billions. He was born in Pittsburgh, Pennsylvania and has two brothers. Mark Cuban's father was an auto upholsterer and his mother was a stay-at-home mom. Cuban would later remark that his early life "was as middle class as you can get," and, just like any other American kid, he spent time at the park playing ball. He eventually attended university (two, as a matter of fact) and obtained a BSc in business. He then went on to serve as a bartender, salesman, and disco instructor—hardly what one would consider the upward path to success. Cuban had one other indignity to add to his resume: He was fired from his sales job. However, this catastrophe was the beginning of Cuban's new lease on life. He decided to embrace the risk of starting his own company. This tiny computer services company, MicroSolutions, became a behemoth that he would eventually sell for $6 million. He is now worth $3.2 billion. Why? In Cuban's own words: " … people were calling me crazy in the computer industry. People were calling me crazy in the systems integration industry… . The more people think I'm crazy and out of my mind, typically, the better I do." Cuban channeled his willingness to embrace risk into opportunities, and accepted uncomfortable change as his leitmotif.

The name "Rothschild" now evokes images of fabulous wealth and a global banking network, but this was not always so. What few know is that the very beginnings of the Rothschild rise were scarred by injustice and prejudice; in fact, most of the family's history has been colored by anti-Semitism. Even from the very beginning, few would have expected the Rothschild family to become a global powerhouse that spans generations. This is because the Rothschilds were Jews—and the Jewish people have suffered from severe persecutions throughout their history. Europe of the 1700s was vastly different than the liberal collection of nations we know, despite the influence of the Enlightenment. The Jewish people in Europe and Russia experienced systematic persecution that was enforced by the governments and embraced by many people. The laws regulating Jewish people were some-what different depending on whether they were in Prussia or Poland, but they were all unfair. For example, Jewish homes or valuables could be seized at any time, their children (and sometimes adults) could be forcibly converted to Catholicism, or they were forbidden from living in large areas of the major cities. Wealthier Jews were often blackmailed and forced to pay excessive fees and taxes. They were prohibited from owning land (an act in 1751 that allowed Jews to own land in progressive England was even swiftly repealed) or engaging in most kinds of trades. That any Jewish family could rise above such systematic persecution is almost unthinkable—yet they did.

The founder of the family, Mayer Amschel Rothschild, was born in 1744 in a Jewish ghetto in Frankfurt. He began as a money changer and eventually rose to become a banker to kings. Despite the anti-Semitic rage of his day, he was able to pass his wealth on to his descendants, who confronted similar struggles in their construction of their financial empire. Mayer had a keen eye for business, a strong love for his family—and a willing-ness to embrace risk. He eventually sent his sons to England, Austria, Italy, and France in an effort to expand and protect the family business and growing fortune. Today, while no one knows the exact value of all the Rothschild holdings, estimates range up to $2 trillion, making them the wealthiest family in the world.

The principles of Strive can be found throughout history, showing that their application is not bound by time or place. Take, for example, Christianity. Christianity was spread by the most unlikely people in the most unlikely of circumstances. Those who are familiar with the Bible will know that Jesus had 12 disciples—they will also know that these men were a far cry from the saintly paintings of them found hanging in museums. Simon and his brother Andrew were in business with their father as fishermen; they would have likely been poorly educated but strong workers. The disciple Matthew would have been even considered a less-likely candidate to be a follower of Jesus: As a Jewish tax collector, he was an outsider to his own people who were being oppressed by the unfair tax policies imposed by the Romans. (The Romans, however, did not have any particular love for the Jewish people, seeing them as a strange nation who worshipped only a single God.) The men who followed Jesus were initially not exceptionally brave souls, either. One of the disciples, Peter, swore that he would never forsake Jesus. However, when Jesus was arrested and things looked bad, Peter not only denied that he knew Jesus, but denied it multiple times.

None of the disciples had an amazing heritage or background, yet these men went on to spread the words of Jesus throughout the Roman Empire—and far beyond. Through their efforts, Christianity took root in the ancient world and has become a belief system with over 2.2 billion followers today. Perhaps the most astounding fact about the spread of Christianity is that rather ordinary people often spread it in the face of incredible persecution. Ancient Christians who spread their beliefs included people who had no status in Roman society, including housewives (Perpetua) and slaves (Onesimus). Not much has changed for

more modern Christianity, either. For example, D.L. Moody, the
founder of the Moody Bible Institute, experienced severe poverty
when he was young and worked as a shoe salesman. Charles
Spurgeon, the "Prince of Preachers," suffered from depression
for most of his adult life. What made these individuals different?
How were they able to achieve so much when they began in such
quiet ways? It was their willingness to embrace risk, even in the
face of death.

You Can Achieve Greatness, Regardless of Who You Are

You will likely never need to stare down a lion in the Coliseum,
but you will face challenges in your life. You will encounter
tremendous opportunities to realize your dreams—but only
if you are willing to embrace risk. Intelligence, economic and
political stature, and social systems of advantages can seem to
give some people a leg up, but they do not guarantee success.
Those who have been most successful have often needed to step
outside their comfort zone to achieve greatness. The difference
between the people in the first group is that they do not challenge
themselves, so they do not attain the same kind of greatness.
Langley was surely successful in his forays into astronomy and
timekeeping, but he failed to create an effective flying machine.
The Wright Brothers were confronted by failure after failure,
lacked funds and fame, but used all of their failures to achieve
lasting success. The Wright Brothers didn't have the support of
institutions, academia, or even the press, yet they managed to take
risks over and over again in order to overcome insurmountable
obstacles to realize success.

I myself am not exceptional. I was born into a farming family
and became one more mouth to feed. My father abandoned

me and my mother before I was three. In South Korea, I was average in just about every subject. When I came to the United States, I struggled with the English language, just like any other non-native speaker. I suffered as a minority in elementary school. My life was constantly full of difficulties—but I think that most people, including you, can relate to that. One of the most difficult struggles of my life occurred not long after my mother and I were harassed in our own backyard. Attending school was a challenge for me, but looking back, I realized that my mother's life was impossibly hard. She had no friends. Her family refused to help her. She spoke no English. Eventually, cracks began to appear in her normal demeanor. I began to notice small oddities that had never been a part of her nature before. One day, when I returned from school, I found that she had moved all the appliances and furnishings to the backyard of our rental. She carefully explained that she needed to do this to be safe. We were then forced to move into an apartment. My mother promptly recruited me to move all of the electric appliances onto the balcony outside because she "knew" we were being controlled through them. My mother's mental state spiraled down from there, her behavior becoming increasingly erratic. I knew something was desperately wrong, but I had no idea what to do to help my mom. I explained the matter to my uncles. A year went by with no action.

One day, I decided I had to do something—I had become very worried about my mom's bizarre behavior. Students were always encouraged to discuss their problems with the school counselor, so in my mind, I directly translated this into "the counselor will help my mom." In the office, I calmly explained my mother's strange behavior, not expecting much to happen. However, I was immediately swept up by child protective services and placed into temporary foster care that very night. The shock and horror of my immediate separation from my mother was almost too much to bear. What made it so much worse was that I later found out that neither the police nor social services had bothered to inform my mother that I had been put into foster care. She spent over a month wandering the streets of the city, desperately searching for her lost son. The pain of being separated from my ill mother, the loss of everything I knew, and the sheer guilt I was drowning in overwhelmed me. When I look back at this time, I still feel the searing pain of loss. But I also know that this was the beginning of the greatest challenge of my life—a challenge that I could embrace and grow from or surrender and fail. I chose to meet that challenge head-on. You can meet your challenges head-on, too. You may not be able to control your background, opportunities, talents, or luck, but doing the things that are most uncomfortable is directly within your control. These challenges and risks are the rich fruit that can feed you on your upward path of success.

5 The Secret Things

Luck? I don't know anything about luck. I've never banked on it and I'm afraid of people who do.

—Lucille Ball, American actress and comedian

The Idea That Successful People Have Hidden Advantages Is a Lie

After completing graduate school, I landed a job at Prudential as part of a new elite business unit. There was a team-building/training exercise where the new hires were sent off for the week to Princeton, New Jersey, to compete in a multiday, gameshow-like setting. Teams would answer questions by being the first to slam a buzzer. Since these new employees were the brightest of the bright, there were few wrong answers given. Toward the end of the competition, my team was in last place. The next day, I would be up at the buzzer representing my team. I was ready. Before the final syllable of the first question died on the host's lips, I slammed the buzzer. Point. The second question was met with the same treatment. Point. On and on, the questions rolled, and I racked up point after point for my team. By the end of the competition, not only had I answered every single question correctly, but I moved my team from last place into first. Everyone on my team left with a trophy.

Lucky in Life?

You might be thinking that I am quite full of myself by sharing this story. After all, maybe it was just good luck that helped me. Maybe all the questions were from my specialty. Maybe the other team leaders were feeling sick. Perhaps people just felt bad for me. Those ideas are, I suppose, all possible. But actually, there was a secret to my outstanding success. And it wasn't luck.

The idea that luck or some hidden advantage leads to success is a lie. Part of the reason this fallacy is so popular is because it takes the pressure off the individual. After all, if success is all just good or bad luck, then you are not responsible for anything. Success then simply becomes something that lucky people attain and unlucky people do not. Certain individuals are doomed from the start, and there is no hope of their success, no matter what they do. This kind of "predestination" ideology is particularly damaging to people in midlife. After all, if it doesn't matter what you do, then the desire to simply do whatever becomes quite strong.

If you think about it, luck involves little risk and very little personal growth. For example, people who play the lottery often see it as a very small investment for a very large possible return. This is also true for many of those who take advantage of free online classes. If they invest the time, then they will be better off, but if they don't, they believe there is no significant loss. However, no one ever "lucks" into an engineering degree or "lucks" into building homes for the poor—everyone recognizes that these types of achievements require dedication, hard work, and perseverance. Not surprisingly, these kinds of activities change your life and make the world a better place for those around you. Athough a particularly good opportunity or a devastating event can have an impact on your journey to personal success, it is not what ultimately determines it.

I know that it can seem like a hard concept to swallow. After all, it just seems as if there are folks who get extremely lucky breaks. Look at lottery winners. They seem to have incredible luck, especially the folks who win big, like Stefan Mandel, who claimed lottery prizes 14 times. Others seem to have terrible luck, like park ranger Roy Sullivan, who was directly struck seven times by lightning. Although any person can experience "good luck" in their lifetime, it does not lead to sustained, lasting success. What is more important is how the individual approaches their "luck."

Take, for example, Violet Jessop, whose notorious bad luck would have made most people paranoid.

That Sinking Feeling

Born in 1887, Jessop was the oldest of six children born to Irish immigrants in Argentina. Her father passed away when she was a child, forcing her mother to move the family back to England so she could work as a stewardess on Britain's Royal Mail Shipping Line. Jessop's dream was to study hard and further her education. However, extremely bad luck intervened. While she was in the midst of her studies and preparing to take her exams, her mother became ill. Since the family had little money, Jessop needed to make a difficult decision: She had to give up on studying and apply for a job. In the early 1900s, there were few good jobs for women, but Jessop eventually obtained a position as a stewardess on the Royal Mail Shipping Line's *Orinoco*. She was a diligent worker and started at the very bottom of the ladder. However, bad luck intervened again: Because Jessop was a beautiful young woman, she was regularly harassed by the men on the ship with requests for favors and even marriage proposals. In order to keep her job and support her family, Jessop began to "dress down" and made attempts to conceal her youth. Her sacrifice and commitment to hard work paid off, and she eventually succeeded in advancing to a position taking care of first-class passengers. Despite the loss of her childhood dream of a higher education, Jessop found the siren song of the ocean a powerful force.

Jessop found a position on the White Star Line's *Majestic* as a stewardess in 1909, and eventually transferred to the company's *Olympic* because the pay was better. Things were definitely looking up. However, in September 1911, disaster struck when the *Olympic* hit the Royal Navy cruiser *HMS Hawke*; although two compartments flooded, the ship was able to make it to port. Although the incident with the Hawke did not end in a horrific loss of life, it was the harbinger of a much greater catastrophe.

Jessop transferred to the "unsinkable" *Titanic*, which, on April 12, 1912, struck an iceberg and dragged 1,503 people—men, women, and children—into a watery grave in fewer than three hours. Amazingly, Jessop was one of the few survivors and rescued one of the infants from the sinking vessel. The sinking of the *Titanic* was a personal turning point for Jessop: She found that she had a new courage and understanding of people.

After the horrors of the *Titanic* disaster, Jessop decided that she needed a change and sought a position with the Red Cross, becoming a nurse around the outbreak of World War I. It was a dangerous time to be on the ocean, since the naval battle was in full swing. On May 7, 1915, the *Lusitania,* carrying more than 1 900 people, was torpedoed by a German U-boat, sending the ship—and 1,198 souls—into the ocean depths within a scant 20 minutes. Since the British government had declared war, it was also able to seize assets in order to support the war effort. During World War I, it took two ships from the White Star Line, the *Britannic* and the *Olympic*. The *Britannic* was used as a hospital ship, and Red Cross nurse Violet Jessop was sent to take care of its sick and injured. On November 21, 1916, the *Britannic* struck a German mine, which tore a hole in the ship that flooded six entire compartments—a death sentence. The damage was so severe that it caused the *Britannic* to sink in less than an hour, despite the desperate maneuvers of the captain and crew. Jessop made it into a lifeboat, but needed to make the risky decision to jump overboard. She was pulled under the keel of the massive ship, where she nearly drowned. She was later fished out of the water and, true to form, good-naturedly tended to the survivors. (Amazingly, only 30 people perished in the *Britannic* disaster: Mostly those who had entered the lifeboats first. The ship was sinking so fast that the tiny boats were sucked into the propeller blades.)

Jessop's memoirs show that the most notable quality of her long life, other than her positive approach to everything, was that she challenged herself in the most uncomfortable ways to achieve her goals. She embraced risk, loved and lost, supported her family at a time when there were few good opportunities available to women—and of course, was a part of some of the greatest maritime events in history. After Jessop went through all of the struggles in her early life, she served on many other oceanic journeys, eventually spending a total of 42 years at sea. She passed away quietly at the age of 84.

Lucky Lottery Winners?

What about those people who have good luck, like lottery winners? Newspapers are chock full of the winning lottery numbers and victors. Every new lottery cycle becomes a new opportunity to get rich quick—but the people who are getting rich are probably not the ones you are thinking of.

It's not most of the lottery winners.

The *Cleveland Times* heralded an uncomfortable fact that rarely makes it into the popular press: 70% of lottery winners go bankrupt. That's right—70%. Not only do they lose all of their winnings, but they also lose whatever they started with before the "big win." The *Times* explained this startling revelation away by pointing out that lottery winners are frequently just average Joes. Since they have little experience in managing such an enormous amount of money, they typically spend it on friends and relatives—who often make frequent and outrageous demands. The *Times* argued that if these people could just hire a management team for their money, they would be able to successfully manage it and achieve their dreams.

But is that all there is to success? Avoid your relations and hire the right financial team?

A lottery win is where the sad story of Bud Post begins. He won an enormous jackpot of over $16 million in 1988, more than enough to allow him to live well. Post's problems were not all related to his money: He had already cycled through multiple marriages and occupations. He even did a brief stint in jail. However, the big win made his life much more difficult. His "friends" and relatives were all very interested in how he spent his newfound wealth. Post's life took a definite turn for the worse. A year after winning, he was about $1 million in debt. An ex-girlfriend sued him to obtain a chunk of the cash. Post was then devastated when his own brother was handcuffed and led off to prison—for hiring a hitman to kill Post and his current wife (wife #6). Post himself spiraled deeper into debt, landing in prison again for shooting over the head of a bill collector. He passed away at the age of 66, a broken man.

Post's life is a sad but common story among lottery winners. Do you think it would have been different if he had a financial team? Perhaps—but only if that team was part of a much larger plan to achieve longer, more lasting success. Success rests on the constant embrace of challenges and risk. Violet Jessop's bad luck did not prevent her from pursuing her career or from discovering her love of the sea. Many lottery winners had tremendous good luck but fail to use their winnings to achieve their dreams. Luck had an effect on these people, but it could not determine their success.

But what about that other hidden advantage: Being in the right place at the right time? Some who believe in the idea of this hidden advantage would say that people like Mark Zuckerberg, Bill Gates, and Steve Jobs were simply in the right place, at the right time, with the right technology. To a certain extent, that may be true—after all, it would have been tough to get Facebook up and going in 1500 BC. However, these individuals, as well as many others, would have been successes regardless of the technology. The technology was merely an outlet for their willingness to embrace change and take risks. There are so many variables outside of you that impact your life. However, attributing success to these external factors fails to show how certain people seem to achieve their dreams.

The Impact of External Circumstances

External circumstances affect you and your path to success, but they do not determine your achievements. Our families, the area we grew up in, the early schools we attended (or didn't), government, and events all have an impact on our lives. It would be crazy to say they don't. A person living through the French Revolution in Paris faced difficult struggles that would be unimaginable to a modern Manhattanite. However, what you do with your external circumstances is critical. You can approach external circumstances in one of two ways. You can choose to be overwhelmed and do nothing. Many do. Or, you can choose to embrace the challenges and take risks to achieve your dreams. You can Strive.

Technology is an excellent example of a powerful external factor that impacts success. All of the Industrial Revolutions created shocking, unimaginable change and opened up new avenues of opportunity and wealth. They had a strong, lasting impact on social mores, hierarchies, and cultural development, and even forced changes in governments. The First Industrial Revolution was driven by mechanization, waterpower, and steam power. Huge locomotives transformed the way people traveled and opened up new areas of settlement and commerce; they also displaced millions, destroyed families and entire ways of life, and forced uncomfortable change in every corner of society. The Second Industrial Revolution was driven by mass production, assembly lines, and electricity. Suddenly, people of all social classes had access to cars, washing machines, and refrigerators. Life became a little easier for many. The Third Industrial Revolution was driven by the advent of computers and the Internet. The desktop computer moved an incredibly advanced technology into the realm of reality for millions. An important impact of the rise of the Internet is the incredible amount of communication that is now possible. Many consider that the Fourth Industrial Revolution is the renaissance in cyber-physical systems and robotics. Although this revolution is still in its infancy, it is already revealing some of its potential impact. For example, automation and cognitive artificial intelligence (AI) are beginning to eliminate the need for bank tellers and cashiers; the jobs of the future will mostly require a new set of skills that includes working with AI and robots. The impact of this revolution will be just as disruptive as the others, perhaps more so, since it raises very important questions about humanity: What will happen to those people displaced by AI? Can we upload our memories into a computer to live forever? Should we use cybernetic implants to enhance our bodies? Are we still human if most of our body is replaced with circuitry?

These revolutionary time periods were all ripe with disruption—and innovation. Washing machines replaced some of the difficult and sometimes dangerous work of laundering clothing. Combines freed up farmers to have more control over their budgets and fields. Voice over Internet Protocol (VoIP) and videoconferencing now allow people to meet others in different countries and engage in real-time video communication. However, what is the real impact of technology on the wealth of individuals throughout the world? Fewer than 1% witnessed their net worth advance into the billions. Even now, with all our advanced technology, there are 1.3 billion people living in extreme poverty (less than $1.25 a day, according to the World Bank's definition).

That may make sense for countries where the average citizen does not have access to clean water (like India and China, where estimates are 50% of the population lives in poverty), much less Wi-Fi, but over 46 million of those in poverty live in the United States, 19.3 million in the UK, and 80 million in Europe. An even starker fact is that only eight people have a combined wealth equal to that of 50% of the entire world's population.

With all the advanced technology we have, why aren't more people successful? Why do so many live in poverty?

Some may attribute success to certain "hidden advantages" beyond intelligence, ambition, and hard work; luck or timing are frequently batted around in break rooms around the world. It's difficult to say that farmers who work from sun up to sun down are not working hard enough or don't have any ambition. Malcolm Gladwell is not the only person to point out the benefits of an intact family, positive culture, and a strong social network, and it is not uncommon to see success attributed to variables outside of an individual. But the idea of hidden advantages bringing lasting success is a lie.

Part of the reason we are quick to believe the lie of the hidden advantage is because it is not possible to really know everything in someone's life. We ultimately do not know what struggles a person has gone through to achieve success unless they tell us or those difficulties are apparent; there are many kinds of physical, emotional, mental, or external challenges people face. I know this from my own personal experience. After I was placed in foster care, I was shuffled around through different families. As a child, I could not understand what was going on around me, but I was so angry. I felt that everything was against me. I was still keeping my grades up, but my rage was beginning to take control of my heart and mind. Although I know that the families who took me in probably tried their best, I always knew that to them, I was the outsider. I never seemed to quite fit in. One of the families that took me in even made very clear distinctions between me and their other children; it became so bad that I actually called the state by myself and asked to be placed elsewhere. This was how I ended up being placed with the Amyx family, who would ultimately help me change my life. Mr. Amyx was tall with a Steven Seagal ponytail, blonde, but almost bone-skinny with a huge potbelly. He was a gentle man who was caring for his wife, who survived brain cancer. He shocked me from the very first. He wrapped his thin arms around me and said steadfastly, "I love you." Enraged, frustrated, and more than a little surprised, I said what any other teen would: "You don't love me! You don't even know me!"

I am thankful to say that I lived to regret these words.

I continued my downward spiral, fueled by my rage. After changing high school, I held a competition with my foster brother to see who could get the lowest grades. (It took a lot of effort to get an F.) I dressed and acted like a thug. I became involved with a gang. My reputation at my high school was shot. However, whenever I thought I had pushed the boundaries too far, I found the truly open arms of Mr. Amyx. By my senior year in high school, I had had enough. This wasn't who I really was. I hit rock bottom and felt the sting of guilt when I remembered my angry response to Mr. Amyx's simple kindness. I completely changed. I studied harder than ever before. I tossed out my old clothes. I began to see that my rage was not toward Mr. Amyx. About a year after I told Mr. Amyx where to get off, I took it all back. And he let me.

When I earned a full scholarship to the University of Chicago for graduate school, Mr. Amyx pushed me to go and follow my dreams. With a new hope and new vision of the future, I plunged headlong into my studies. Mr. and Mrs. Amyx believed in me and supported me through my struggles. You could say that it was good luck that I was placed with the Amyxes, but I believe that it was more of an opportunity—after all, I could have continued on my downward spiral, blaming everyone for my problems. Even when I attended college, I don't think I completely understood the impact of Mr. Amyx's genuine, enduring love for me until that terrible day when I could no longer have it.

I know that it's hard to ignore luck. We all have anecdotal evidence of it in our own lives: That time we just happened to make the train before it began to storm or a friend who happened to find $20 on the street when he desperately needed a ride home. The only problem with luck is that it may not be as good as it seems. Any kind of luck, good or bad, cannot be sustained or relied upon. The luckiest among us, lottery winners, may become extremely poor.

Many Advantages, No Success

The argument for some success is that the person was in the right place at the right time. However, this is a poor argument for success. This is because success depends on a continuing, sustained development of the person, rather than a one-time deal. It is what the person has done before and does after an opportunity that matters. No matter who you are, if you have not struggled, taken risks, and improved yourself, the opportunity to achieve greater success will pass you by, sometimes with catastrophic results.

Rehoboam (973–915 BC) was a prince with a legendary pedigree. His grandfather, David, was the subject of much Israelite pride and known for his prowess in battle and word. His father, Solomon, was adored as the wisest man to ever live, and many claimed he was also the richest. Even visiting dignitaries, such as the Queen of Sheba, praised Solomon's great wisdom and wealth, proclaiming:

> It was a true report which I heard in my own land about your words and your wisdom. However, I did not believe the words until I came and saw with my own eyes; and indeed the half was not told me. Your wisdom and prosperity exceed the fame of which I heard. Happy are your men and happy are these your servants, who stand continually before you and hear your wisdom! (1 Kings 10:6–8)

Rehoboam was raised in the royal household and was named Solomon's heir. He also had the advantage that no other king did: He still retained many of his father's wisest advisers, men who had been at the helm during Israel's golden age when the temple was being constructed using pure gold. It was shortly after Solomon's death that opportunity came to Rehoboam. The timing, as they say, was perfect. The situation was also perfect. What Rehoboam did was blow it.

The opportunity came in the form of a delegation from the tribes in the northern part of the kingdom. During Solomon's time, major construction projects were ongoing, so the people of the north were heavily taxed in terms of resources and labor. With Solomon on the throne, there was no chance that these issues would be resolved, but with a new ruler, the delegation thought it had a chance. They begged the king to lighten their burdens and promised to serve him loyally.

Solomon's counselors advised Rehoboam to grant the men their petition. They reasoned that it would quickly create a good bond between them and the new government. It is very likely that the people in the north would see Rehoboam as a new man, a kind of father figure very interested in the welfare of his people.

Rehoboam listened to the old men's counsel and then did what all young people do—he asked his friends. The problem with Rehoboam's friends was that none of them advised Solomon. None of them were the sons of kings, and none of them knew how to rule a kingdom. What they did think they knew was that Rehoboam had tremendous power, and may have been looking for a way to help him consolidate it. They gave Rehoboam their kingdom-ending advice.

Rehoboam not only told the delegation that he would not grant its request but foolishly added that he would make its burdens heavier. The people of the northern part of Israel could bear it no more. They broke with the southern tribes, a disaster that would have long-lasting consequences.

Rehoboam was the right man in the right place at the right time who did the wrong thing.

His foolishness led to the critical split of Israel into the northern kingdom of Israel and the southern kingdom of Judah. It was also the beginning of the end for the entire kingdom. The two states were not as strong separately as they were together, so when the Assyrian war machine began its campaign of slaughter, the northern kingdom quickly capitulated. Although the Assyrians were turned away through a last-minute intervention at the very gates of the capital of the southern kingdom, Jerusalem, it was not the last ravage of war the southern kingdom of Judah would see. The ultimate loss was yet to come. The Babylonians took Jerusalem, razing Solomon's temple (the first temple) in 586 BC. Occupations by the Persians and Medes, Greeks, and Romans eventually followed, and the remaining Jewish people were kicked out of Jerusalem in the second century AD. Israel ceased to exist until returnees who were scattered throughout the world officially reclaimed it in 1948.

Ursula Burns, Risk Taker

When Ursula Burns went from the secretary's desk to the C-suite, there may have been some people who pointed out her incredible luck. They might even have pointed to the unique timing, claiming that Xerox was focusing on being more inclusive in its leadership.

They Would Be Wrong

Burns's story doesn't start in the C-suite. It doesn't start behind the executive assistant's desk. It's doesn't even begin at Xerox. It began with a filthy tenement in New York City, where drunks and drifters would camp out under the main staircase. Burns's family struggled to make ends meet, and her early life was scarred by poverty. Her mother raised the children alone by running a small day care center in the apartment and tackling odd jobs. Burns repaid her mother's hard work by studying and obtaining a mechanical engineering degree at the Polytechnic Institute at New York University. She wanted to earn a master's degree, as well, and sought out and obtained an internship at Xerox. In 1981, she became a full-time employee in the product development department. She experienced no meteoric rise. Every day was full of hard work; Burns tackled challenging problems and stretched herself to find new solutions. But she kept at it. She began to explore other departments at Xerox, moving through the company with persistence.

And Then It Happened

While attending a seminar on diversity, Burns was appalled when the speaker could not even address a straightforward question about why the company was pursuing diversity in its hiring practices. Burns faced the risk of speaking out—it could result in some heated debate. Rising from her seat, she called the speaker out about his "lack of conviction." After a brief interaction, the incident was over—at least, until Burns found out that she had just gone head-to-head with Wayland Hicks, an executive VP of Xerox.

She Assumed Her Career Was Over

In fact, her risk paid off. Hicks met with her several more times and then invited her to work as his executive assistant, which at first insulted Burns. She was a highly trained engineer with decades of experience. She had no intention of doing what she saw as "stepping down."

Hicks, however, was quick to point out the real reason for the move: It would allow Burns to get real leadership experience. Burns accepted, and the rest, as they say, is history. She became the first African-American female CEO of a Fortune 500 company. Burns received no handouts in her rise to the top—her willingness to embrace risks and perseverance in the face of adversity are what made her an overwhelming success.

The Real Hidden Advantage

We have seen that every successful person has embraced struggle and risk-taking. It is simply that it is not obvious—the veneer presented to the outside world often conceals a deep pool of experience. Even when a person seems to be experiencing pure luck, it is still not the case. Remember Stefan Mandel, the man who won the lottery 14 times? A winner with that much luck almost seems unbelievable.

Mandel's success was anything but luck.

He was a talented Romanian mathematician who spent years poring over complex mathematical research papers in order to develop his system. The system he created was a mathematical monster that covered about 8,000 pages. At the time, he was only trying to crack the code to win the Romanian lottery, which was a much smaller prize with fewer possible number combinations than those typically found in the United States. Mandel could not even use his entire approach for that lottery, either—he simply lacked the cash. However, after revising his strategy to fit his pocketbook, he purchased blocks of lottery tickets and took home his first prize in 1964. Mandel initially moved his family to Israel and then Australia. There, he took another risk: He tried to find investors to help him reap the harvest of many more state lotteries. His entire plan involved a serious devotion to mathematics, the risk of purchasing large blocks of lottery tickets before the deadline, and the need to raise cash from willing investors. The Australian government eventually made it impossible for Mandel to keep winning the lottery (he won 12 times there). His final victory? Getting the International Lotto Fund, his Australian investment syndicate, to pony up $5 million to pay for five million combinations in the Virginia state lottery, the vast majority of the possible seven million combinations of numbers. The final jackpot? $28 million.

By now, I hope you have shaken off the idea that outstanding luck can lead to real, lasting success. I think that you may have also guessed how I was able to successfully answer every single question before anyone else could lay a finger on their buzzers. I prepped for the questions just like anyone else. And then, late at night when everyone else was asleep, I crept down to the competition room. There, in the pale moonlight, I spent hour after hour pressing the buzzer. I had studied my competition and knew they were all extremely smart. But I also knew that quickly pressing buzzers was probably not a skill they had acquired. I took the extra step of building up my speed in this one area, lost some sleep, took the chance that someone would see me (embarrassing!), and became a hero to my small team. The real hidden advantage that every single person has is the ability to strive. Embracing well-considered risks, large and small, has helped make me into a success. And it can help you, too.

6 Disrupt Yourself

The secret of change is to focus all of your energy, not on fighting the old, but on building the new.

—Socrates, Greek philosopher

Use Self-Disruption to Attain Success

Have you ever noticed how some entertainers have the power to reinvent themselves? Justin Timberlake, for example, morphed from a teenage heartthrob into a producer, restaurant owner, and philanthropist—and was startlingly successful in every role. What has made Timberlake, and others like him, so successful at reinventing themselves?

There are successful individuals who have both innate and acquired talents and skills, riches, a good background, and a positive outlook, but none of these are enough to create and sustain success. True success comes from that which is uncomfortable: Disruption.

"Disruption" is frequently batted about in tech circles to describe the sudden, incredible change brought about by a technology or action. For example, the Internet disrupted how we do business, communicate, and obtain information. Before the Internet, we usually talked face-to-face or through phone calls, we might have dropped a letter in the postbox for grandma, and we would walk to the public library to spend a few hours among the stacks to find information. Disrupting yourself means to embrace uncomfortable change. In this chapter, I will show how disruption leads to success and how you can start using it to achieve your goals.

The most successful individuals, corporations, organizations, and nations have disrupted themselves repeatedly to stay relevant and valuable. This is because being comfortable leads to complacency. Success requires constantly introducing experiences that make you uncomfortable or challenge you to improve yourself and achieve lasting success. The principle of disruption can be seen all around us—even inside of us. Take, for example, the development of your muscles.

Disrupting the Body: Building Muscle

What does it take for you to improve your strength and tone your body? A healthy diet can boost your immune system and give you the energy you need to thrive. But it won't necessarily make you physically much stronger. You could, however, start lifting weights—not so many that you appear to be a flesh-colored bunch of grapes—but enough so that your bone density increases and your muscles grow. Research has shown that lifting weights increases your muscle mass and heavier weight training leads to more muscle.

Weight training involves stressing the body beyond what it usually does. This does not include stressing your body so it is damaged—no doctor or trainer would ever tell you to do that—but it does include pushing yourself a little more every time to improve your abilities and strength. Heavier mechanical stress imposed on muscles results in higher amounts of metabolic stress, and this stress generates a greater activation across a significant percentage of muscle fibers. There are three ways to make your muscles grow: Muscle tension, muscle damage, and metabolic stress. Muscle tension occurs when you start lifting weights that are heavier than those you lifted before. Muscle damage is a by-product of that exercise—working your muscles naturally introduces some damage and inflammation in the areas that were stressed. Finally, metabolic stress is your body's reaction to that damage.

Now, it may seem obvious that if you lift the same amount of weight week after week in the same way, you may initially get a little stronger, but will eventually plateau. This is because your body adapts to your weight lifting routine. In order to get stronger and become more fit, you need to not only lift heavier weights but you also need to lift them in different ways. To make your whole body stronger, you don't just do weight training with your arms. You also need to lift weights with your legs and torso. You may find that lifting weights is making you stronger, but you are still being beat to the ice cream truck by grandmothers with canes. Lifting weights makes you stronger—but walking or jogging can improve your heart rate, increase your endurance, and make you quicker. All these approaches to strengthening your body involve you constantly improving. Doctors agree that weight training and aerobic exercise, like jogging or kickboxing, can significantly improve your health. (We will go over health and how it impacts your success in Chapter 10.)

Strength training sounds great—and it is for most of us—but it is uncomfortable. It requires that you regularly engage in stretching your body a little bit further than before. Sometimes, you might feel achy. There are times when you may also injure yourself if you push too hard. But in the end, this uncomfortable exercise yields dividends in terms of your health and wellness. Plus, when you have more energy, you can accomplish more—in some cases, much more—than you could before you began to exercise.

The example of muscle growth beautifully explains how we need to think about exercising our "disruption muscles." In order to experience incredible success, we have to transform ourselves continually through perseverance and striving toward more expansive goals. We adapt and grow by creating stress that is greater than the previous threshold we have already adapted to. This can be done by going outside your comfort zone, taking risks, and continually changing your habits so that you can push yourself into new territories that you can't otherwise reach at your current level.

Disrupting the Individual

It is not only our bodies that utilize the principle of disruption. There are people all around us who also practice this idea to various degrees. Serial entrepreneurs are an excellent example of people who are constantly challenging themselves.

Shooting for the Stars

There are two kinds of people who can get away with saying that they want to "make humanity interplanetary": Sci-fi writers like Isaac Asimov, who foresaw an extremely well-developed human civilization in his classic *Foundation books*, and Elon Musk, who has a plan to colonize Mars and is developing the technology for it, too.

Few entrepreneurs can draw a crowd or a dollar like Musk. Perhaps his most enduring characteristic is that he is not afraid to embrace risk or uncomfortable change; it is something that his sister, Tosca, identified about their entire family in an interview with *Esquire magazine*: "Without sounding patronizing, it does seem that our family is different from other people. ... We risk more." Musk was born in 1971 in South Africa, and in his youth became a great fan of comic books where heroes saved the world. At a young age, Musk wanted to achieve great things, and he started to find ways to accomplish his goals. Musk began his college work in Canada, but transferred to the University of Pennsylvania to complete two degrees, one in physics and one in economics. He briefly attended Stanford, but found that the allure of the computer was strong. Musk dropped out of grad school and founded Zip2. (This company sold map and business directory software to news agencies.) Zip2 was sold to a division of Compaq in 1999 for over $300 million. Musk himself pocketed a cool $22 million. He turned his keen eye to the emerging technologies supporting fintech and was soon busying himself with his newest pet project, X.com. X.com eventually evolved into PayPal, a global financial powerhouse, which Musk sold for $1.5 billion. He did not become complacent, instead embracing another challenge, one that echoed from his childhood—namely, space travel. Initially, Musk attempted to purchase rockets from the Russians, but realized that they were not serious about dealing with him—a challenge that he would need to face repeatedly on his quest to reach the stars. Instead, he struck out on his own. SpaceX (Space Exploration Technologies) was started to make space travel cheap and reliable. (Musk's SpaceX Dragon craft has already had a successful run to the International Space Station.) Musk took ownership of Tesla in 2008; he has been working to return more manufacturing jobs to the United States and push the boundaries on environmentally friendly vehicles. SolarCity is another part of Musk's vision that creates renewable energy systems, and Musk has been following up on his commitment to build the Hyperloop, a super-fast train that can cut a two-hour trip down to 12 minutes. (Early testing is going on to create a Hyperloop in Dubai.) Neuralinks, Musk's newest venture, is a company dedicated to creating the link between man and machine through the brain-computer interface. Musk also started a charitable foundation in 2002 to help others find solutions to issues in a range of areas, including space exploration, renewable energy, education, and childhood illnesses.

Space exploration. Renewable energy. Brain-computer interfaces. Childhood disease. Any one of these areas could consume a lifetime of effort and energy, yet Musk has been able to achieve them before he started to go gray. His ability to disrupt himself, identify new challenges that interest him, and then pursue them has made Musk king of the entrepreneurs. But he is not the only one.

The Power of O

You cannot buy groceries without glimpsing her broad smile. In the publishing world, her word is gold. In 2016, *Forbes* identified her as the #2 richest self-made woman in the world ($3.1 billion). She's so famous, she only needs to go by her first name.

Oprah

Oprah Winfrey, the queen of daytime talk TV, actress, producer, author, tastemaker, and self-help guru, was born in 1954 in

Kansas. The woman who is now one of the world's richest self-made billionaires grew up in abject poverty. She lived briefly with her mother and then her father, who encouraged and supported her dreams. Winfrey began seizing opportunities: She was the first female African American co-anchor on Nashville TV. Winfrey eventually moved on to another station, where she began to mine her talent for deeply connecting with others. Her first foray into talk radio in Chicago shot to the top of the charts. In 1985, Winfrey showed her acting chops in *The Color Purple*, and won nominations for a Golden Globe and an Academy Award. In 1986, she launched *The Oprah Winfrey Show* (the highest-rated show of its kind in television history) and Harpo Studios, and became one of the few entertainers in history to produce her own program. She would later go on to act in and produce the show *The Women of Brewster Place*.

Winfrey has a keen understanding of people and an insatiable thirst for challenges, going so far as to completely reinvent her mega-hit TV show. Instead of only focusing on particular problems, like abuse or addiction, and how to solve them, she began to redirect her energies toward helping people improve their lives. Her book recommendations were so powerful that a new marketing term was named after her: the Oprah Effect. (To give you an idea of how much influence Winfrey has, consider the following: 59 of the 70 books that appeared on her Book Club list shot up to the top 10 of *USA Today*'s bestsellers list.) She started the Oprah Winfrey Network (OWN) to provide a broader platform for her ideas; as cofounder of the cable channel Oxygen, Winfrey was able to rapidly expand her audience. Winfrey also turned her star power toward publishing in 2000, and her *O Magazine* currently enjoys a circulation of over 2 million. In partnership with Flatiron

Press, Oprah's co-authored books on everything from spirituality to healthy eating have enjoyed a strong readership. Oprah also briefly returned to radio, and Oprah Radio, a talk channel on Sirius/WM radio, ran from 2006–2014.

Philanthropist Winfrey has long been a proponent of "giving back." She has supported over two dozen charities, most notably her Angel Network. Unlike many charitable organizations, 100% of the donations were used for projects such as schools (55 schools in 12 countries), grants to organizations that help women and children in difficult circumstances, and disaster relief (the foundation helped build homes for people after Hurricanes Katrina and Rita).

Oprah is the leading lady of personal disruption—she has constantly embraced risk and change to achieve her goals—but has always had a generous, open hand for the downtrodden. To provide a little insight on Winfrey's generosity, *Forbes* noted that in 2008, Winfrey gave away $50 million—more than five times that of any other celebrity that year, a whopping 20% of her salary that year. (In 2016, she gave away over $40 million.)

Reinventing Your Business

Some of the most iconic companies have completely reinvented themselves through disruption. They have managed to bring hundreds (and even thousands of people) together to strive for greatness—with outstanding success.

Consider GE: In 1892, it began as a power company. By the 1940s, GE was building trains alongside its stable of home appliances. The company currently runs multiple research labs, two TV networks, and a number of other types of business. However, this was no easy task: GE needed to invest in its researchers and employees, encourage innovation, and constantly seek out new challenges in order to stay viable and grow.

I would be remiss if I did not mention the grand old lady of tech: IBM. Although many people today recognize Big Blue as the undisputed champion of enterprise server solutions, what they may not know is that when the company first incorporated in 1911 as the Computing-Tabulating-Recording Company, it was making products like scales and cheese slicers; it employed 1,300 workers. In 1935, IBM garnered the government contract to keep Americans' employment records as part of the new social security act. By the 1970s, IBM was already riding the rising tide of interest in computerized technology, and is credited with developing one of the precursors of the ATM. IBM also manufactured personal computers, but found that in the 1990s, it was being soundly beaten by competitors; the company steered its efforts away from personal computing to focus more on business. In 1997, IBM proved again that it was willing to adapt to the changing world of technology: Its emergent-AI Deep Blue supercomputer beat world chess champion Garry Kasparov. Deep Blue's capabilities highlighted the immense potential of the supercomputer and the beginning of IBM's hot pursuit of AI. Now, IBM's Watson is a marvel of technology, an AI with almost unlimited potential that is being used to underpin the company's successful evolution into an enterprise solutions provider. IBM had over 380,000 employees as of 2016 and a market cap value of $143.5 billion as of October 2017. Not bad for a centenarian that used to hawk cheese slicers.

Maybe you already have a business. Perhaps it has enjoyed a modicum of success, too. But you find that you have still not reached all your goals, and some of them now seem further away than when you first started. Strive is not just something for the individual—it can be used more broadly to impact groups of people at nonprofits, small businesses, and even large conglomerates. Now is the time to apply the principles behind Strive to your organization.

Disrupting Your Nation

Disruption works on a global scale, as well. The United States is certainly one of the most famous historical disruptors—it re-created itself from a tiny handful of colonies dependent on a superpower to itself becoming a superpower. The struggle for independence was costly and involved tremendous hardship: Families suffered irreparable losses and whole ways of life were upended. However, the transformation resulted in the creation of a nation that welcomes those from all over the world and offers opportunity to those willing to strive for their goals. America is not alone in its national disruption. We are living in an exciting time when national disruption is occurring all around us.

Korea is a terrific example of how disruption can lead to success. There are really two Koreas: North Korea and South Korea. They operate under completely different governments and ways of life. Originally, Korea was a single nation, but it experienced a heartrending civil war in the 1950s that forever separated families and created two distinct approaches to government. South Korea is what most people think of as Korea today.

South Korea is a strong example of how embracing change and taking risk can completely disrupt and transform a country. When most people think of Korea these days, a rich plethora of images pop into their minds: Samsung, Hyundai, K-pop, K-drama, spicy kimchi, savory barbecue, stunning architecture, cosmetics, and fashion. It's hard to imagine South Korea any other way—but in the 1960s, it was one of the poorest nations in the world. The story of how Koreans transformed themselves from a third-world country to become an economic powerhouse is mind-boggling—but makes sense in light of how willing the entire nation was to disrupt itself to achieve lasting success.

South Korea has few natural resources; ironically, its neighbor to the north has a cornucopia of natural riches. North Korea has not only failed to prosper, but has needed outside aid to stave off the worst of its famines and natural disasters. South Korea only redeclared itself a nation in 1948 after its forced annexation by the Japanese in 1910 (although Korea itself has existed for thousands of years—the people of Korea have been sculpted by the millennia, maintaining their own distinct culture). It is impossible to do justice to the complex history of the Korean peninsula in just a few sentences, but it is fair to say that the people of South Korea have struggled, not only with their pursuit of an open and fair government, but also with the whiplash changes brought about by technology, increasing wealth, and foreign trade. Whereas the northern government clamped down more firmly on its people, forcing them to shut out even the most rudimentary technological innovations, the southern government promoted a higher standard of living, encouraging trade and the development of the infrastructure. Although South Koreans started with little more than perseverance and hope, they managed to outstrip their northern brethren by embracing new ideas of commerce and technology. The formation of private companies was encouraged, and construction projects were seen as part of the nation's future. The government itself began investing in various industries, reasoning that what was good for industry was good for all the people. Embracing these types of economic change was risky, in light of the nation's few natural resources and precarious relationship with the North, but it catapulted South Korea into an economic tiger.

Now, Korea is known for manufacturing the chips used in most of the portable electronics devices at your business and in your home. Much of the recent architecture in Seoul is futuristic, like its Lotte World Tower, Olympic Stadium, Urban Hive, and World Trade Center. As if the view of the city's buildings was not enough, the look on the street is cutting-edge modern. Seoul is a fashion mecca like no other, and it can boast this because it encompasses its own strong textile industry. Dongdaemun, a complex in Jongno district in Seoul, is the world's largest fabric market—hot fashion trends can literally be conceived of one day and on the streets the next. Korean cosmetics have taken the world by storm: In 2015 alone, the nation's cosmetic companies exported more than $2.64 billion worth of their products. K-pop and Korean drama stars have immense global audiences. (This may be partly due to Internet sites like DramaFever, which translates songs, movies, and TV shows for non-Korean audiences.)

However, Korea's incredible success was achieved through great hardship. From 1910 to 1945, Korea was occupied by Japan, and the nation suffered under its rule. In 1953, the nation was divided in a bloody civil war. The South Koreans were ruled by a succession of strongmen and then eventually elected leaders. The path to becoming a tiger economy was not a smooth road. South Korea had to deal with the constant incursions and threats from the North, including outright kidnappings, bombings, and sabotage. It also needed to find its voice in the emerging global economy, no small feat for a country about the size of Indiana.

There have, of course, been terrible struggles and difficulties, and there are many more challenges to come. For example, South Korea has decided to maintain an American military presence, which is extremely controversial inside and outside of the country. Social roles are in flux, as the traditionally Confucian society adapts to modern life. There are issues with the power of the chaebols, large Korean conglomerates that were part of the construction of modern Korea, but which may be holding the nation back from developing further economically. Safety issues have been a constant source of concern.

I was born in South Korea (near the DMZ) in 1973 and lived there until I was nine years old. I can tell you that the changes I see today are astonishing. In the year I was born, strongman Park Chung-hee was still in power. Children attended school in military-inspired uniforms complete with hats. Farm animals shared the roads with buses and a few cars. There were no skyscrapers and certainly no Korean wave. My mother and I lived near the DMZ, and there was a strong military presence in the area. (Needless to say, I became well-acquainted with SPAM and corned beef.) In 1961, the average income in Korea was $72, but in 1973, it had already climbed to $2,840. To get a little perspective on these numbers, consider that the average income in the United States was $5,700 in 1961 and $12,050 in 1973. Fast-forward to 2016: South Korea has a fully elected government. The most recent data available showed that per capita income was about $33,000 (from the OECD data).

More interestingly, South Korea is a model for what can happen when an entire nation pulls together to embrace risk and face challenges together: It is the first country in the OECD that went from being a recipient of aid to a donor. From its Korean International Cooperation Agency (KOICA) to being one of the top nations sending out Christian missionaries in the world, Koreans have channeled their success into worldwide generosity.

Korea is not alone in its journey to transform itself. When Mohammed turned his gaze to Mecca, he may have been able to glimpse the amazing future of his homeland. In 1932, Ibn Saud carved out his kingship on the Arabian Peninsula, a harsh desert land. The discovery of oil in 1938 birthed the Arabian-American Oil Company (Aramco), which soon became the nation's greatest source of wealth—and global controversy. Not much changed in Saudi Arabia until King Abdallah began instituting reforms that began the disruption that has birthed the modern nation of Saud. He allowed women, who had few rights, new employment opportunities, courted foreign investment in the nation, and began to support privately owned companies. A banner year was 2005: It was the first time any Saudi voted for a government official at the municipal level. By 2015, women obtained the right to vote and be elected to municipal posts. Abdallah's disruption provoked myriad responses, some from traditionalists and others who thought the king did not go far enough. However painful the disruption was, it was setting Saudi Arabia on a new path to the future. (In 2017, King Salman ordered the reform in a royal decree to issue drivers' licenses to women.) The nation has now implemented its National Transformation Plan, an ambitious program with 346 goals, all targeted at sculpting Saudi Arabia into one of the world's technological powerhouses. Its goals include massive disruption, such as shifting a percentage of corporate ownership from the government to the private sector, strongly enhancing its research and development of advanced technologies, and progressively embracing healthcare initiatives. The plan's motivation is to break the nation's costly reliance on oil, improve the country's living standards, and move it into the modern era. There's big pain in these big gains: Saudi Arabia currently imports about 60% of its needs, the state owns significant assets, and its people suffer from lifestyle-related illnesses and a poor education system. Mohammad bin Salman bin Abdulaziz Al Saud, the Crown Prince of Saudi Arabia and First Deputy Prime Minister of Saudi Arabia, is the driver of change, but it will be up to all of Saudi Arabia to win. The latest national disruption is an announcement of a $500 billion plan to build a megacity near the Red Sea to enhance the business and industrial zone that links with Jordan and Egypt, the biggest effort yet to free the kingdom from dependence on oil exports.

Starting Successfully

I hope that, by now, you are convinced that the principles of Strive can work for you—and others. The disruption brought about by uncomfortable change and risk can help you achieve your goals. However, just taking any risk or changing anything may not get you where you need to be. The first thing you need to do is plan what success will look like for you and then do the legwork to understand how to achieve your goals.

Earlier, I developed a simple path to Strive using its letters:

S—Set a goal.

T—Think about how to get there and plan for success.

R— Risk: Embrace it, expect it.

I—Insights, or what did you learn from your uncomfortable change or risk?

V—Verify progress.

E—Enhance yourself, mentally and physically, with safe bio-hacking.

Let's take a look at the first two letters here.

(S)—Set a Goal

What do you want to accomplish with your life? How will others remember you? What is really important to you? If you have read this far, you probably already have several goals in mind. Some of them may be personal, some professional. These ideas can help you create your life mission statement. The creation of your mission statement is the first step towards fully understanding and achieving your goals.

One of the most important aspects of this process is having clarity in your personal-life-mission statement, since it is the over-arching driver of your goals. It fundamentally identifies who you are and what you want from life. Your personal statement should be derived from a considerable amount of thought. Your statement will be influenced by what you enjoy doing, what you want others to understand about you, the people you admire, the legacy you want to leave behind, and how you will impact the world around you.

Businesses and nonprofits often have mission statements to help clarify what they stand for and what they hope to achieve. Some sample statements are

"Spreading ideas."

—TED

"[The American Red Cross] prevents and alleviates human suffering in the face of emergencies by mobilizing the power of volunteers and the generosity of donors."

—American Red Cross

"To prepare young people to make ethical and moral choices over their lifetimes by instilling in them the values of the Scout Oath and Law."

—Boy Scouts of America

"To combine aggressive strategic marketing with quality products and services at competitive prices to provide the best insurance value for consumers."

—AFLAC

"To nourish and delight everyone we serve."

—Darden Restaurants

"Dedication to every client's success. Innovation that matters—for our company and for the world. Trust and personal responsibility in all relationships."

—IBM

What might a mission statement look like for you? It all depends on what you want to achieve in your life. If helping others is important, it should be in your mission statement. If innovation is key to your life, it should be in your mission statement. Mission statements should include broad, overarching ideas. They can be as long or as short as you want.

Some sample personal mission statements are:

"I want to support others and help them achieve their goals."

"I will do unto others as I would have them do unto me." (Yes, the Golden Rule is a mission statement.)

"I will use my natural abilities and learned skills to improve the world around me."

"I would like to advocate for positive change for the poorest among us."

"I want to help my family grow and enjoy the beauty of life."

After you have developed and written a mission statement (yes, write it down and put it somewhere you can see it), you can effectively set goals. You might find that after you conceive of your statement that some of the goals you originally developed do not really match what you wrote. That's fine. You may even find that your personal mission statement will evolve over the course of your life. That's normal, too. As we get older (and hopefully wiser), we begin to see ourselves and the world in very different ways. Revisit your personal mission statement regularly to ensure that it is truly what you want to achieve.

Although you will only have one mission statement, you can have multiple goals. This is because your mission statement is basically your guiding philosophy for your life: It is the overall summation of your hopes and legacy. Your goals are short-term and long-term steps toward realizing your overall philosophy.

You define your goals in light of your mission statement. First, what is one long-term goal? Let's use one of the preceding sample statements.

"I want to support others and help them achieve their goals."

One long-term goal here might be:

"I want to build and staff a school that helps children use technology."

Now, what would short-term goals look like?

"I need to get a degree in technology and education."

"I should get donations to build the school."

(T)—Think About How to Get There and Plan for Success

Now, how can you reach your goals? Reaching your goals involves planning and thought. Research how to achieve your goals and then revise them, if necessary. In our example, you might find that starting a school does not require that you have a degree—but it does involve getting many people involved who have financial means. This might change your short-term goal.

The first and most obvious place to start your research is the Internet. Find out everything you can about your goal. However, do not just rely on the Internet. Make lists of people who have already accomplished it or something like it. Reach out to them—politely. Building relationships with people who have accomplished something similar is fundamental to your success. Don't be afraid to ask. Your local library will have books and other resources that provide a reliable foundation for your goals. Online platforms such as LinkedIn can help you locate people who might be able to help your reach your goals.

After you begin your research, you will begin to find that there are obstacles and challenges to completing your goals. Make lists of these, and include details. What challenges do you need to overcome? How can you do that? Who can help you? What are some small steps you can take right now to meet your goals? What are some long-term steps to meet you goal?

For our example, some challenges may include

"Money—schools require millions of dollars to buy the land, get permits, put up the building, arrange for a staff, market the school, recruit students, and provide maintenance."

"Understanding—many people will not understand why a new school must be created when there are already existing schools."

Although the Strive method may seem clear to me now, I admit that when I was younger, I did not quite understand how to achieve my dreams. Instead of considering what I truly wanted out of life, I found myself copying what others were doing to achieve what they thought was success. I did not carefully think about what my life was about. Part of this might be because developing a life mission statement is uncomfortable. It requires serious introspection, and quite honestly, I carried a lot of my rage and frustration from my youth into adulthood. It seemed to me like the world was against me. I was frustrated by leaving my homeland and integrating into a new culture. I was enraged by the loss of my mother and the blatant racism I experienced. I hated bouncing around foster families, never quite fitting in. Then, when it seemed like I had found a real home, it was all ripped away from me. While I was in my third year at college at a summer fellowship program at Carnegie Mellon, I got the call: Mr. Amyx was terminally ill. I came back home immediately, my heart in my throat. The man who I will always love and respect as my father was slipping quietly away. I wanted to stay by his bedside, but he loved me more than his own life. "Go back, finish your studies," he said. I left with a heavy heart. Not long after I returned to my studies, I lost my father.

Mr. Amyx helped me to understand the importance of family, and he gave me the strength to see that my life mattered. It was this understanding and strength that eventually helped me to see how I could make a difference in the world and finally attain my dreams. He molded my philosophy in powerful ways. Determining your philosophy may be a struggle at first, and figuring out how to carry out that mission is not always easy. However, they comprise the strong foundation for your journey to your success.

And now the really hard work begins.

7 Abandoning Your Comfort Zone

Pearls don't lie on the seashore. If you want one, you must dive for it.

—Chinese proverb

Risk It

If you have read this far, you already understand that although many successful individuals have innate talent, a good background, connections, or "luck," it does not mean that any one of those factors ensures success. These intrinsic and extrinsic advantages are nothing without risk-taking and uncomfortable change. Only by taking well-thought-out risks can you create repeatable success. You must challenge yourself to become better—better as a person and better in your professional life. Challenges involve stretching yourself, getting outside of your comfort zone, and embracing uncomfortable change—and risk—as a way of life.

Not just any risk will result in the kind of aspirational success you need. There are many ways that people embrace risk, but they are not all beneficial. For example, you have no doubt heard a parent make the comment that "If all your friends jumped off the bridge, would you jump too?" (Yes, your parents did have a good point.) Doing something because others are doing it is a terrible reason to embrace risk. Another reason people take on risk is because people they respect or answer to are forcing them to do it. This approach to risk usually occurs at school or at work when a manager or instructor may be hinting (or openly telling you) to do something that is extremely uncomfortable for you. The best reason to embrace risk is because it moves you toward your goals. Taking chances does not mean "checking your brain at the door." The wise advice from Proverbs is still relevant today: "Without counsel, plans go awry." Counsel can come in different forms, but it is the foundation of your research for your goal. Before taking any kind of risk or embracing change, carefully consider how the action will move you toward your goal. Your objective when taking a risk then is to pursue something that you believe in that will ultimately help you achieve your goal and live out your mission statement: It is a calculated risk.

Comfort Zone Versus Twilight Zone

What does risk look like? The truth is that risk is different for everyone because our wants and philosophies vary. Regardless of who you are, the risks that you take should align with your mission statement and help you to achieve your goals. A few risks will only happen once. For example, accepting a scholarship at an overseas university is usually a once-in-a-lifetime choice. Overcoming your fear of public speaking is a journey that may last your whole life.

We have now moved to the third part of Strive:

S—Set a goal.

T—Think about how to get there and plan for success.

R—Risk: Embrace it, expect it.

I—Insights, or what did you learn from your uncomfortable change or risk?

V—Verify progress.

E—Enhance yourself, mentally and physically, with safe biohacking.

I have compiled a very brief list of risks that can help people achieve their goals. I am sure that you can come up with many more. What kinds of risks do you think you will need to take on your journey to success?

- Changing careers
- Overcoming one of your fears (such as a fear of heights, public speaking, or spiders)
- Starting your business
- Taking on more responsibilities at work, at home, or in the community
- Volunteering at a food pantry
- Relocating or temporarily living elsewhere, far away from what you're most familiar with
- Taking the first step to mend a broken relationship
- Getting out of an abusive relationship
- Supporting missionaries
- Getting to know new people in different racial or social-economic groups
- Beginning a family
- Adopting a child

- Overcoming a disability
- Speaking out against evil
- Running for political office
- Being more honest with yourself and others
- Transforming a business
- Changing a nation
- Changing society

Taking calculated risks has a powerful impact. If you think that striving to achieve your goals will have little impact on the world around you, you should think again. Sometimes, just following what you believe to be right can make a world of difference to others.

Risk-Taking Impacts the World

"Who is Malala Yousafzai?"

In a U.S. classroom, this question might be met by a few raised hands, but it certainly wouldn't be met with silence and terror. But on October 9, 2012, on a school bus loaded with teen girls, these words brought the horror of death. No one pointed to Malala, but they didn't have to—stolen glances gave the 15-year-old away. A gunman approached the young girl, rage blazing in his eyes. He raised his gun and shot her in the head at point-blank range.

What led up to that horrible day in 2012? Malala was living with her family in the Swat Valley, Pakistan, when the Taliban began to struggle for control of the area in 2007. Malala's father founded several schools, and was a powerful advocate for education—for both girls and boys. However, the Taliban's campaign against the education of women went far beyond a peaceful exchange of words: It razed 400 schools. Many families were afraid to send their daughters out of the house, fearing they would be killed or kidnapped. The area was a war zone, with bullets, suicide bombers, and militants a constant threat. Malala saw the chaos all around her and decided that enough was enough. Her father recognized her tremendous courage and perseverance, so he encouraged her to do what she believed was right. On Pakistani TV in 2009, Malala publicly decried the violence against women from the Taliban, asking why they should be able to take away her right to an education simply because she was a woman. Malala's efforts in Pakistan gained her and her passion recognition. She received a nomination for the International Children's Peace Prize in 2011 and was awarded Pakistan's National Youth Peace Prize. She also gained recognition from another, unwanted, source: The Taliban. Their leaders understood the tremendous threat Malala's commitment presented and called for her blood.

The Western media turned its focus to the chaos in the Swat Valley. The BBC was looking for an insider's view of what was happening in Pakistan, but found it was difficult to get anyone to cooperate. The Taliban's fearsome grip was silencing even the bravest of souls. That was when Malala's father encouraged her to write about her daily life for the BBC—a bold turning point for the young woman. Malala's simple testimony about the daily suffering she endured over her education had a powerful impact. Her story took a sharp, dark turn when it was revealed that Malala was the writer of the column. The Taliban increased its threats against her family, warning that Malala was a target. When Malala and her family refused to back down, the Taliban stretched out its bloody hand in an attempt to silence her forever.

But, as you know, Malala's story did not end on that bus. Instead, she moved from a local stage to the global one. Although her injuries were severe, she was airlifted to a hospital in England and received treatment. Malala has since recovered and become a powerful voice for change and education. On her 16th birthday, she spoke at the UN in New York about peace and the importance of education for all children. The fund she set up with her father has allowed her to travel to different areas of the globe to speak out for children and women's rights. In 2014, she was awarded a Nobel Peace Prize, the youngest person to ever receive it. Her book, *I Am Malala*, details her life and struggles; perhaps the most amazing thing about Malala is that she has suffered for taking risks, but she did not become bitter.

Malala still fights for a child's right to an education, and her story continues to inspire people around the world. But she is not alone in her ability to face incredible risk. There are many other people, some who will forever be nameless, who have challenged and defeated those who attempted to do great harm. They have taken incredible risks and not only changed themselves, but also the world forever. Take, for example, those who are now referred to as the Righteous Among Nations.

Everyone is familiar with the horrors of the genocide that took place during World War II. We also know that there were many regular people who took risks to hide, protect, and evacuate the Jewish people at that time, such as Corrie Ten Boom (whose family hid Jews in their home, and whose incredible story appears in *The Hiding Place*) and Chiune Sugihara (who issued thousands of visas to Jews fleeing their homeland against the orders of the Japanese government). What many do not know is the incredible risk incurred by the Polish people who aided, protected, and evacuated Jews. Poland was Hitler's first major target, the first nation to suffer the blitzkrieg. It was also the only nation occupied by Germany where the Nazis issued the terrifying edict: Any person caught aiding the Jews would not only be subject to the death penalty, but their entire family would be executed as well. However, this edict did not stop Drs. Eugeniusz Łazowski and Stanislaw Matulewicz. "The basic duty of a physician is to preserve life," Łazowski would later tell journalists, "and this was a way of saving lives."

Łazowski had much to lose: He knew that he was not only risking his own life, but also that of his loving wife and beautiful daughter. However, the young man found that he could not allow the rampant slaughter of innocents. Together with Dr. Stanislaw Matulewicz, he hatched an incredibly daring plan that involved an important aspect of psychology: Fear. Łazowski and Matulewicz understood the Nazi mindset very well. Simply put, they had a petrifying fear of germs and disease. And few diseases struck fear into the heart like typhus, an incurable infection with symptoms of fever, chills, rash, and mental haziness. Without modern treatment, it is fatal. Matulewicz found that by injecting healthy people with the dead typhus bacteria, he could make it appear that someone was infected, although the person would not exhibit any symptoms of the disease. Of course, the doctors could not inject the Jews with the bacteria—Jewish people infected with typhus were summarily executed by the Nazis.

Instead, Łazowski and Matulewicz took an incredible risk: They injected their non-Jewish patients in the areas surrounding the Jewish families, effectively creating a ring of infection.

This forced the Nazis to quarantine the entire area, including the regions with a significant Jewish population. The quarantine prevented the Nazi soldiers from entering the Jewish villages to remove the Jews living there.

The doctors began their fake typhus epidemic in 1942. Incredibly, no one seemed to notice that the death toll in the area was not rising until 1943. It was then clear to Polish collaborators that no one was dying from the epidemic—and they alerted the Nazi overlords. The eye of the German state focused hard on Łazowski, but he enjoyed a bit of celebrity since he was a young doctor who was willing to treat patients even in the most dire of circumstances. A German medical team was dispatched to inspect the area and do some fact finding about the "epidemic." Fortunately, Łazowski knew they were coming. In another risky move, he assembled the oldest, sickest, and dirtiest members of the community and placed them in filthy hovels. He planned an outsized reception for the Nazi doctors that included plenty of food and alcohol. Then, he showed them to the hovels, carefully reminding them of how typhus was spread and congratulating them on the enormous risk they were taking to themselves. Needless to say, the Nazi doctors were quickly satisfied by the "epidemic" and fled the area, leaving Łazowski and his innocents safe until the end of the war.

Both Łazowski and Matulewicz took incredible risks to achieve what they knew to be right. If the men had been discovered, they and all those who cooperated with them would have been executed. However, their gambit paid off: It has been estimated that the doctors saved almost 8,000 lives.

Not all risks are the same. We all live in different circumstances. Sometimes, the risks that are taken do not come from an oppressor, but come from the environment.

Journey to America: In Search of Religious Freedom

Every American elementary student gets the same general overview of their country's history: In 1620, the Puritans boarded a ship for the New World in order to enjoy religious freedom. When they landed, they found some friendly Indians who helped them survive in their new environment. For most of us, this is where the story ends.

What we don't know about the people who came over on the *Mayflower* is that they faced down stunning odds to find a new homeland. The hardy souls that made that voyage in 1620 not only braved a long sea journey (over 2,700 miles in about 66 days), but also the threat of violent pirates, slavery, disease, and the possibility of starving to death.

The journey did not begin well. Originally, the *Mayflower* had a companion ship, the *Speedwell*. The ships departed from Southampton in early August, but had to return to port because the *Speedwell* kept leaking—this was repeated until the pilgrims gave up completely on the *Speedwell* and began their perilous adventure in September of 1620.

When the Mayflower eventually landed at Cape Cod in the winter of 1620, there had only been one death on the ship. This may have seemed to be a fortuitous sign, since crossing the sea would have undoubtedly claimed many more lives. However, what the pilgrims did not count on was the fact that the ship did not land anywhere near the Jamestown colony. It made land much farther north—600 miles—in what is now Massachusetts. Even with help from friendly Indians, the pilgrims faced a gruesome winter. When the ship made landfall, it was far too late to actually plant any crops, much less have anything grow in the harsh New England climate.

Scurvy stalked these wary souls, stealing their dreams and many lives before the warmth of summer arrived.

Only 58 of the original 102 souls from England actually survived the winter, yet in the spring of 1621, not a single pilgrim opted to return to Europe. Instead, their commitment to living free allowed them to build, plant, improve their relationship with the local Indian tribes, and eventually celebrate that very first Thanksgiving—they were expressing their thanks to God and their hopes for a new life.

The stories of great heroes, like Malala, are inspiring because they took enormous, life-threatening risks. But most people in first-world nations will never risk life or limb to pursue their dreams or achieve success. There are many kinds of risk, and the kind of risk depends on the person and their circumstances. Although you can be inspired by the success of others, you should never see it as the measurement of your own success. This is because every person's life is different. No two people have the same personality, circumstances, or challenges. Stories of success are the signposts on your own journey. They are the cheerleaders that support you through the tough times, motivating you to stay strong and keep pressing on. The risks you take in your journey toward success will look different from that of most of the stories that appear in this book (and hopefully very different from that of James Buchanan and Czar Nicolas II). The kinds of risk you will probably face will be in your personal or professional life. And there are few things more risky than business.

Risky Business

Risk always involves getting outside of your comfort zone. I began to take real risks with my professional life when I first realized that I was not achieving my goals. It all started after I had worked in wealth management for several years. I always thought that I would be a millionaire by the time I was 30. Somehow, that hope was eluding me. I realized that what I really needed to do was follow my dream that began its formation in my childhood—I wanted to have my own business. I decided to leave the comfort of a steady paycheck and jumped headlong into my very first entrepreneurial endeavor.

The L'Amyx Tea Bar

It was a hip little cafe that was funded largely by home equity loans and family funds, and was nurtured into profitability by myself, my wife, and my sister-in-law. I have always had a skill for identifying rising trends long before they take off, and I sensed that people were ready for something new—a restful cup of tea. The tea bar was years ahead of its time, with offerings of high-quality loose leaf teas from around the world. Not only did the tea bar offer a taste of Russia, Korea, China, India, and Japan, but it catered to that one area where most people prefer to spend their money: Experiences. We offered a relaxing welcoming environment paired with authentic Japanese tea ceremonies, introducing the power of Eastern relaxation to the overdrive of Western life.

It Was a Success.   Everything was great. We were riding high on the success of the dot-coms around us. The shop was voted Best of the East Bay several times, I was interviewed by SFGate and Asia Week, and our steady stream of eager customers had ready cash and open minds.

And Then It All Came Crashing Down.   As you may have already guessed, the dot-com bubble burst, taking with it thousands of jobs and almost all our customers. The downturn could not have happened at a more difficult time, and the falling fortunes of the tea bar had a powerfully negative effect on me. Since I still held on to so much anger from my youth, I was not always pleasant to be around. I was hypercritical, not only of myself, but of others. I'm ashamed to say that I did not treat my sister-in-law very well, and instead pushed her harder than ever to help make the business successful. Eventually, my behavior was too much for her, and she quit. My wife was pregnant with our first child. The landlord would not budge on the rent, which was about $10,000 a month. We couldn't make the mortgage payments on our house. I was overwhelmed by the thought of possible failure. Without a steady income, I could not even begin to think about how I could take care of my family. Everything looked bleak. My sense of self-worth plunged. I needed help, and there was really only one person I could turn to.

That's Right, My Sister-in-Law

With my hat in my hand, I humbly approached her and asked if she could buy me out. It was an incredibly difficult thing for me to do. I had mistreated her while we worked together and was bitter when she quit—even though it was my fault that she left. To my surprise, she agreed to run the tea bar again.

As soon as she took over the business, things began to improve. A business line of credit suddenly opened up, and I was able to keep the café doors open during the transition. My sister-in-law completely revamped the tea shop and drew in more customers. After I left the helm of that business, it went on to enjoy a decade of profitable years under her care.

Starting my first business was a risk that was both a failure and a success. The business almost disappeared under my watch.

I almost destroyed my relationship with my wife's sister. My family almost went bankrupt. But it was a success in that I realized, deep within, that I was broken. My behavior during the whole process was damaged and damaging. I needed help. It was then that I began another risky venture, one that took me far beyond my comfort zone but that resulted in a victory that was unimaginable.

Start-ups are risky, and small businesses are all about risk. But what about companies that are already established? Taking risks pays off for them, as well.

Amazon

Jeff Bezos, whether you love him or hate him, is the ultimate risk taker when it comes to revolutionizing his business. Bezos built his reputation on striving for what seems like the impossible. In a 2014 *Fortune* interview, Jeff Bezos stated, "My job is to encourage people to be bold. I've made billions of dollars of failures at Amazon.com, literally billions. ... Companies that don't embrace failure and continue to experiment eventually get in the desperate position where the only thing they can do is make a Hail Mary bet at the end of their corporate existence." And Bezos has had some spectacular failures.

Amazon started in 1995 as an online bookstore. It then reinvented itself to stay alive, becoming an online retailer in the 2000s. Although Amazon began to see a brighter future, the road ahead was still quite bumpy.

For example, the Fire Phone smartphone went up in smoke, an auction site failed to draw many bids, Endless.com ended, and then Amazon took a $970 million hit for video streaming site Twitch. (How many Twitch videos have you watched lately?) But

Bezos was willing to risk—and fail—in order to strike gold. His perseverance paid off. Amazon Web Services (AWS) launched in 2006. This was not just stretching outside the company's comfort zone, it was launching into the Twilight Zone since it was completely different from everything the company had accomplished. However, as of 2016, AWS is so much a part of the digital economy that most start-ups use it, as well as big names like NASA. When hackers want to get attention, they use AWS attacks to shake everyone up.

Although Bezos has not faced down literal death, he has faced and embraced struggle and uncomfortable change and achieved outsized results. What makes Bezos unique is his utter commitment to embracing failure as part of the ultimate victory—Amazon is worth an estimated $89 billion today and does not seem to be slowing down. Bezos is not the only person who does—or can do—this. You can too.

Personal Risk, Incredible Growth

As I mentioned before, there are many kinds of risk. I would like to emphasize this so you do not fall into the trap of comparing yourself to others. Your success is entirely personal. You might speak out or act against something you know is wrong. You may take risks with professional issues, such as starting a company or moving it in a completely different direction. There is another, extremely challenging kind of risk: Personal risk. These are very uncomfortable ways of helping yourself become a better person. These risks involve the hardest step of all—changing yourself.

Buzz Aldrin. Gwyneth Paltrow. Winston Churchill. Emily Dickinson.

You probably noted that these are all famous, accomplished individuals. You probably did not know that they all suffered from depression.

Depression and mental struggles are rarely discussed when we talk about success. Who wants to get dragged down? But it's unrealistic to ignore mental issues. They are very real. Unfortunately, although many celebrities are trying to reduce the stigma associated with mental health issues, it is still quite strong. Facing mental health challenges is a risk. It means admitting to yourself that you are flawed. It means admitting that you need help. Few problems strike at your core like admitting that you don't have all the answers or that you cannot fix yourself. Don't think that only the weak have mental struggles. You would be surprised by the high achievers who struggle with deep personal issues.

Into the Light

She's been named one of the most beautiful women in the world. She's taken home many awards, including an Academy Award and Tony. She's graced the big screen in over 30 movies, and has lent her superstar power to musicals and plays.

Yet in April of 2011, Catherine Zeta-Jones knew that something was very wrong—and instead of trying to hide her suffering, she reached out for help. It was a stunning admission from a woman who seemed to have it all: A loving husband, healthy children, a powerful career, wealth, and great beauty. Zeta-Jones experienced a bout of depression after helping her husband, Michael Douglas, with his cancer diagnosis and treatment. She checked herself into a rehab center to help cope with the overwhelming aspects of her life. Zeta-Jones has gone public about her struggles, and has highlighted the fact that sometimes the most challenging part of life is managing our inner world.

Zeta-Jones is just one of many people who seem to have it all, but suffer quietly. I understand the suffering that she has gone through. I have trudged down that dark road myself.

My failure at the tea bar fully laid bare my intense emotions from my childhood. My fears and disappointments seemed to crystallize in front of me. I had always thought I was strong, but I would find myself breaking down for no reason. I felt that I needed to meet all challenges in life with stoicism, but could not control my stark criticism of others. I fought back against depression on a daily basis—utterly and completely alone. As a Korean man, there were certain things that were unacceptable, and admitting to struggling with anger or emotions was not acceptable. Worse, I was about to commit one of the greatest unspoken taboos of my homeland: I decided to see a psychotherapist.

Although I felt some initial reserve about going, I knew that my problems would not suddenly evaporate. Nothing I had done over the years had brightened the darkness or quieted the fears. I was terrified that these problems would grow with age, and I did not want these dark remnants from my past to control my future. I had a beautiful family. I had hopes and dreams. Although I had found God when I was younger, I felt like I was not being useful to Him. I wanted more from life, and I knew I needed to get help—immediately. I was in therapy for about three years. During that time, I found that I could name my problems. Fear of abandonment. Depression. Rejection. Hatred of myself. A hypercritical spirit. I was afraid of other people, afraid to walk into a room full of strangers because I felt they would be judging me. Part of my healing came from understanding my problems.

Although I am not perfect, therapy was what I needed to really begin changing myself from a man consumed by anger to a man free from his past. I highly recommend therapy. Never let the people around you, your past, or your fears hold you back from getting the help you need. Striving to reach your goals is all about helping you attain and become a success, both in your professional and personal life. Taking care of your mental well-being is as important as risking it all to achieve your dreams.

Taking risks is incredibly scary. I mentioned my earlier fear that I would be discovered practicing for the Prudential competition. Imagine if someone saw me! A few of my colleagues may have respected me or not thought much about it, but others would have surely said unkind things to my face or behind my back. Office gossip can be a terror.

Risk looks different for everyone, so do not compare the risks you take to achieve your dreams to what others risk. Some risks will be incredible, like mortgaging your house to start your business, changing careers, or moving to another country to teach English. Others will be smaller risks that help you move to a better place to either embrace greater challenges or make you a stronger person, like learning to say what you want or speaking up in a meeting. You have, no doubt, already taken some of these smaller risks. I have, too. When I was first placed into foster care, I stayed with a loving couple who made sure all of us foster kids went to church every week. One Sunday, the youth leader asked if any of us knew any verses.

No One Raised a Hand

I paused and thought carefully. I was raised Buddhist, and my first exposure to Christianity had been through some missionaries in

South Korea. I did not know much about the religion. But did I know any verses? Surely I must have learned something. I strained to come up with an idea.

Then it hit me.

I definitely knew one verse, that one verse that I had seen everywhere. I looked around the room.

Not a single kid was raising a hand.

Could it be that they were too scared? I was terrified of talking in front of so many people, but the answer was dancing on the tip of my tongue. At last, I couldn't take it anymore. I raised my hand and dutifully repeated the verse that was poetry throughout every place with running water in California.

"If it's brown, flush it down. If it's yellow, let it mellow."

There was a stunned silence in the room. Suddenly, the entire group erupted in laughs and cheers. Later, I discovered that the youth minister was actually asking for Bible verses.

I hope that you are encouraged to take risks big and small to help you realize your dreams. It is only through struggles that you can climb higher and become more than who you are. What happens after you take chances? What if they succeed? What if they fail? Let's take a look at what to do next in Chapter 8.

8 When the Going Gets Tough

Fall seven times, stand up eight.

—Japanese proverb

Pairing Risk with Perseverance Is Necessary for Your Ultimate Success

Have you ever been unemployed? Many of us will experience at least a short period of unemployment in our lives. It's one of the worst situations you can find yourself in. Not only does your family struggle because you lack work, but your self-esteem takes an enormous hit. You wonder if you have any value as a person. Looking into the eyes of your suffering spouse or children is soul-shattering when your only thought is how to keep a roof over their heads. I have gone through tough periods of unemployment. I was devastated by my failure with my tea bar, and I moved from contract to contract. The times we needed to live off of our savings were difficult personally and financially—but enlightening. It was this tough time in my life that showed me a very important aspect of success: Perseverance. I took risks in order to support my family and tried to stretch myself to get outside my comfort zone. However, it was not just "hanging in there" that helped me eventually reach my goals. Rather, it was the reflection on what I had learned that helped me to persevere, which led to a kind of "informed perseverance." I did not keep trying to do the same thing with no positive results. Rather, I thought carefully about what my risk had taught me and then used it to help me pursue my dreams.

One of the insights I gained from my yo-yo employment history was that people were not simply hiring a "strategy consultant" or "product manager." They were hiring "Scott, the man who will create value for my customers" or "Scott, the man who will 'bring his A game' to my product line." They weren't hiring a name or title: All employers want to hire a passionate, vital person who will turn their talents to supporting their company or helping them attain a goal. This insight completely changed how I was pursuing my dreams of success. I eventually paired this insight with some calculated risk to launch myself into a brand new business. This approach to analyzing the outcome of your risk and staying on your chosen path can help you attain real success, too.

Staying the Path, Eyes Ahead

Taking risks isn't enough. It's taking risks and failing, but having the courage to get back up, fine-tune your approach, and then trying again. You must think carefully about the risk you plan on taking. After you take the risk, you need to analyze it. What insights did you gain? These insights can help you stay on the right track.

We have now moved to the fourth part of Strive.

S—Set a goal.

T—Think about how to get there and plan for success.

R—Risk: Embrace it, expect it.

I—Insights, or what did you learn from your uncomfortable change or risk?

V—Verify progress.

E—Enhance yourself, mentally and physically, with safe bio-hacking.

In Chapter 7, we discovered that you must challenge yourself to move outside your comfort zone and embrace risks to achieve success. Here, we take a look at another part of Strive: Insights. Ultimately, insights will help you achieve your goal because they function in two ways. They help you see what your risk made you learn and they help you persevere. Nothing is more demoralizing than failing and not understanding why. If you take a risk and it fails, you need to consider why it failed. This will help you understand how to achieve your goals. After you take a risk, you should think about what you hoped to gain from it and what you actually attained from it. If you think your risk moved you closer to your goal, you will find that it is easier to persevere. If not, you must reconsider what kinds of risk you need to take to reach your dreams.

When you first begin to pursue your dreams, you will fail. Some people will fail a little; others will fail a lot. Some of these failures will be quite painful. In order to persevere, you must understand what your goal is. If your goal is unclear or it's something that you find you have lost the motivation for, you will give up. This is why so many people fail—they give up.

Insights Help You Reassess Your Goals

January and February see huge upticks in the gym population. By the time March rolls around, many of those gyms are empty. Why don't people stick with it?

It's because it's usually not something they really wanted to do in the first place. Maybe some of the women felt terrible when looking at media-enhanced images on Instagram or Facebook, so they decided they would be "bikini-ready" by summer. Maybe some of the men thought if they could just hit the gym a few times a week, they would look like "The Rock" and attract some attention. Or maybe a doctor told them that they needed to exercise to get their cholesterol levels in the "right" range. Whatever the impetus, the real drive did not exist inside the individual, so the plan fizzled out. Besides, exercise is hard, often boring, and does not always yield the quick results we hope for. (Actually, exercise alone may not accomplish much of what we hope for.) Since it is difficult to see overwhelming results immediately from exercise, some people feel that it is not worth the time or effort.

Part of the problem is that these people did not really want to achieve an exercise-related goal. But another issue is because those who give up do not think about what they have done to achieve their goal and how to improve their chances of succeeding. For example, if you go to the gym and lift five-pound weights every day for a week, you might feel that you have worked very hard—but you might see no results. It would be easy to be discouraged. However, if you think about what you were doing, you may understand that you need some additional information about how to get those giant muscles you see in magazines. You would find that spending an hour or two with a professional trainer can help provide greater insights into how to improve your health.

People do not only fail to achieve goals in the area of physical fitness, either. A whopping 75% of college students will change their major at least once before graduating. Why do so many students change their minds about what their goals are? In a review of research about college students, Liz Freedman of Butler University noted that students were largely choosing majors based on "influence and assumption" rather than thinking about what they wanted to accomplish with their lives. Instead of thinking carefully about what they want and researching how to achieve it, they rely on what others around them say or how they feel at a particular time. Money and respect are also motivators in choosing a college major. As I mentioned earlier, fame and money can be the by-products of your goals, but they can never be goals. Since some young people erroneously follow a career that boasts big dollar signs, they are disappointed to find that it is not only something they are not good at, but also something that they care little about. This is the antithesis of success. A good example of this can be seen in medical schools. In some households, the high-achieving children are expected to become a doctor (or another well-respected, high-paying career such as lawyer or engineer). The parents are the drivers of the career choice, and they push the idea because they want their son or daughter to be well-off and respected. Most parents love their children and understand how difficult the world is when funds are limited or people look down on you. The children may not have a strong opinion about an area of study or they may want to pursue another career. Whatever the child's desires, they typically put it on the side because they want to please their parents. And so off they go to pursue a career they don't enjoy—and it shows. They may have good grades, but since their hearts are not in it, they are not true successes in life.

In college, many students take the risk of attending school and getting into classes in their chosen major—and some are very disappointed. However, the outcome of this risk allows the student to either clarify their goals ("I do not want to study physics, I prefer chemistry") or provides insight into their goals ("I didn't know I needed to take calculus to be an engineer"). This insight, which resulted from their failure, can actually help them move closer to their dreams—if they are willing to persevere and take other risks to achieve their desired goals.

There are people who have taken risks and then found that they could no longer pursue their passion. Sometimes it was due to outside forces, but other times, it was because their risks helped them realize where their real passions were.

The Blind Man Riding on the Back of a Blind Tiger

Like Aladdin, Jack Ma has a knack for making his wishes come true. Ma is the founder of Alibaba and one of the wealthiest men in the world ($3.9 billion, #33 on Forbes list of the richest people in the world). If there is any modern businessman who understands perseverance, it is Jack Ma.

Born in September of 1964, Ma was a child of the dawning nuclear age in China (in October, strongman Mao Zedong would order the first test of a nuclear bomb in Xinjiang) and a son of the Cultural Revolution (a massive ideological purge that resulted in the death of 1.5 million people). When Ma was 12, he developed an insatiable passion for learning English and poured himself into it. Every day for eight years, he would ride his bike to a local hotel to give free tours to the foreign tourists just so he could practice his English language skills. This perseverance paid off—but not immediately. In 1985, one of the families he had helped in China asked him to visit them in Australia. Ma's world was completely overturned by what he found there. He later recalled: "Oh, my God, everything is different from what I was told." Ma realized that the things he had been taught while growing up were not entirely accurate. This new insight set Ma upon a new path—but it still did not translate into instant success.

Many students in the United States might apply to colleges once, right after they graduate from high school. Ma failed the Chinese college entrance exams twice before getting into Hangzhou Teachers University. He then applied for graduate school at Harvard University, not once or twice, but 10 times. He was rejected every single time.

Shortly after graduation, Ma sought out employment in various places, but every application resulted in disappointment. No matter where he turned, he struggled to find work. But Ma's unfailing desire for something better led him in a different direction. In 1995, Ma went to the United States as the interpreter for a business team—and that was when he was first introduced to the Internet. Ma briefly owned a company that partnered with China Telecom but found that his true passion was on the Internet. In 1999, Ma launched Alibaba. The company suffered so many setbacks that Ma actually referred to it as "1,001 mistakes." Today, the e-commerce monster that is Alibaba is worth an estimated $200 billion. Ma, well known for his humility and positive attitude, is not stingy about sharing his massive wealth. In 2015, he became China's #1 philanthropist by donating shares valued at $2.4 billion to his charitable trust. Ma is particularly interested in helping solve the problems with the environment, health care, and education in his homeland.

A Cinderella Story

"My story is like a Cinderella story in that I worked hard and beat the odds." This was how mogul Dottie Herman described her own ascendance to the top of the tough real estate market. The President and CEO of Douglas Elliman presided over a blockbuster year in 2016, when the company sold $24.6 billion worth of real estate. Her personal net worth is estimated at over $270 million. Looking at Herman's success, it might be hard to believe the incredible difficulties it took to get there.

Herman was born in Brooklyn, but the family moved to Long Island. She was the oldest of three children. Everything changed for Dottie when she was 10 years old. Her parents had taken the whole family skiing in Vermont, and on the return trip, the unthinkable occurred. The family was involved in a horrific car accident. Not only did the accident leave Herman with seizures and her father disabled, but it took the life of her mother.

That was when Herman swore she was going to make something of herself.

The road to success was long and hard. Herman had to step up to care for her younger siblings, an experience that forced her to grow up very quickly. When Herman was younger, she aspired to be either a teacher or an actress—but she did not get to follow either path. Instead, she worked hard and entered Adelphi University to work toward a degree in financial planning. It was then that Herman became pregnant with her daughter, Christine. Many women would have dropped out of school, but Herman knew that she needed to push forward. It was a struggle to be a single mother and focus on her studies, but Herman persevered. After graduation, she obtained a position at Merrill Lynch in the

1980s, which was eventually bought by Prudential Long Island in 1989.

Herman, no stranger to risk, decided to invest in her own vision. She knew that she could run Prudential, except she completely lacked the funds to buy it: Prudential was going for a cool $9 million. In a masterstroke of business savvy, Herman persuaded Prudential to loan her the cash for the sale. Known for her candor and positive attitude, Herman took the company to new heights of success. In 2003, Herman and her business partner scooped up the Manhattan brokerage Douglas Elliman for $72 million. In 2014, Herman earned accolades from Gotham Magazine as one of New York's Most Influential Women. In 2015, she took home the Innovator of the Year Award from Inman for her unique, tech-savvy approach to the real estate market. Herman has also made a point of giving back to the community. She has mentioned how many people have helped her during the difficult parts of her life, such as when her mother passed away and when she was a single mother. She is actively involved with the Katz Women's Hospital of the North Shore, Southampton Hospital, the American Heart Association, and the Every Woman Matters Walk.

Insights Help You Persevere

When you take a risk and evaluate its outcome, you have already moved yourself in a positive direction. Even risks that fail can help you see where you went wrong, so you can try again, or point you in an entirely new direction where you can enjoy greater success. There are many stories of those who failed repeatedly but used their insights to enjoy success.

Taking the Long View and the Long Road

When Katheryn Hudson decided she wanted to be a singer, there was one thing she did not do: Give up. Born into a family of devoted Pentecostal Christians, Hudson spent much of her early life traveling. The family was far from well-off, and sometimes found themselves at the local food bank. Hudson knew she wanted to sing, and eventually began to perform for her parents. This was perhaps one of her first risks: Sharing her love of singing with her relatives. Hudson's parents listened seriously to her, and then encouraged her to get voice lessons. This first risk provided a powerful motivator for the young woman: Other people thought she had talent and believed in her. There was no turning back.

Hudson got her first opportunity to spread her wings with gospel music. She cut her first album, *Katy Hudson*, at 16, with songs such as "Trust in Me," "Faith Won't Fail," and "Search Me." Unfortunately, the album basically went nowhere, selling only 200 copies before the recording company closed, leaving Katy to start over at Square 1. However, this risk showed Hudson that her desire to become "the next Amy Grant" may not be the best way to pursue her passion, so she began to explore other options to take her closer to her dream of becoming a singer. Most importantly, Hudson needed to express her own style and her own words.

Hudson understood the value of an education and so completed her GED at 15 so she could focus on her music. She moved into singing secular tunes, and in 2004 signed with Java, which was affiliated with The Island Def Jam Music Group. The deal went nowhere. However, this opportunity was definitely an encouraging failure: Hudson made strong connections in the music industry and was eventually able to sign on at Columbia records. Hudson was then asked to sing with the group The Matrix, which she readily agreed to. The group worked on getting the album ready for almost two years. After much struggle and perseverance, Columbia dropped her contract.

Although Hudson felt the sting of the lost contract, she had a much clearer vision of her future. It did involve hardship, as she sang backup vocals and took a number of jobs to help support her dream. Hudson was then signed on at Capital Records in 2007 and released her first hit album, *One of the Boys,* in 2008. The rest, as they say, is history. Katy Hudson, or Katy Perry as you may have guessed, has moved from success to success, garnering awards and becoming the best-selling artist of all time. Her hard work and ability to take risks and learn from them has made her an American icon.

The entertainment business is tough, but if there is anything tougher, it is politics.

Coming from Nowhere, Going Somewhere

Alexander Hamilton, who would become the first Secretary of the Treasury and set American monetary policy, experienced significant hardship, but never flagged in his pursuit of his goals.

His humble beginnings would haunt him for the rest of his life. His parents were not married when he was born in 1757, largely because his mother was already married to another man—Johann Michael Lavien—with whom she already had a child. Hamilton's father, not well-off himself, eventually abandoned the tiny family, leaving Hamilton's mother to fend for herself and two young sons. Hamilton's mother moved close to her wealthier relatives, who helped her set up a small store.

Although Hamilton would have likely wished to attend school, he helped out with this store, making it prosperous. In 1768, both Hamilton and his mother fell desperately ill; within an hour after his mother passed away, members of the probate court appeared in front of the sick boy to claim all his mother's property. This was because Hamilton and his brother were never considered legitimate children.

Peter Lytton, a cousin, eventually took both boys into his home to care for them, but tragedy struck when Lytton, plagued by failed business adventures, ended his own life. Merchant Thomas Stevens took in the young Hamilton, who obtained a position as a clerk with one of the men who used to supply goods to his mother's store. This position brought Hamilton considerable knowledge—and knowledge was what he so greatly yearned for. Hamilton wanted to learn and leave his island home, but there seemed to be little hope for that. Still, every moment that was not spent at work was employed in his own directed self-study. After a hurricane wreaked terrible destruction, Hamilton wrote a letter to his father that was published in the local newspaper by Hamilton's mentor, Hugh Knox, a minister and journalist. This letter was what made local leaders decide to educate Hamilton in the American colonies. However, even in this regard, Hamilton was at a disadvantage; he could not be educated by the church in the colonies since he was illegitimate. Instead, he went to a private school, and eventually attended college. However, his studies were interrupted when the British occupied the city. It wasn't until 1782—years after the War for Independence—that Hamilton would study on his own and pass the bar.

But what Hamilton learned was that he had a passion for government. He turned to the power of his pen to encourage his fellow Patriots. Hamilton then took a risk by joining the New York Provincial Artillery Company, and climbed through the ranks, eventually garnering the attention of George Washington. After the war, Hamilton would find himself enraptured by politics, and would become a champion for a new constitution. He wrote the majority of the *Federalist Papers,* and went on to shape the economy of the new country.

Fail Again and Again

How strongly do you believe in your dreams? Would you say that you would be willing to fail 50 times? How about 5,000 times?

James Dyson was willing to fail more than 5,000 times to eventually bring his invention to the world. Each failure brought him new insights that encouraged him to press on. In 1978, Dyson was engaging in a familiar ritual practiced in modern homes across the globe—he was tearing apart his vacuum cleaner to understand why the confounded machine was not working well. Dyson carefully considered his wayward appliance and realized that a great vacuum could be constructed using "cyclone technology"—a system that uses centrifugal force to separate particles from the air. Dyson had actually utilized this type of system before in an industrial cyclone tower for a factory. It took Dyson five years to realize his dream of creating a better vacuum cleaner, but that's only part of the story. He actually developed over 5,000 prototypes—all somewhat close to what he needed but still not quite right. When his working prototype was ready, Dyson was sure that it would be a hit with businesses.

But he was dead wrong. In fact, while Dyson's creation was certainly effective, it would have destroyed the current business model for most vacuum cleaner companies. They sold the machines cheaply and then made money off the recurring demand for vacuum cleaner bags. Dyson's vacuum completely sidestepped this moneymaker and in doing so, sidestepped many companies that could have launched his creation.

Still, Dyson was convinced that his vacuum could benefit others and at last found a willing market in Japan. In 1991, it won a design award. Dyson's living room struggle had come to an end, when, in 1993, he launched his own business to create and sell vacuum cleaners. Today, Dyson is worth an estimated $6 billion. (You could say that Dyson really cleaned up.)

Although Dyson's dream was to make your house clean, some people have the desire to simply explore and understand the world around them.

Into the Heart of Darkness

Fighting an angry crocodile on the Congo and confronting a charging leopard sound like action scenes from a modern movie. Would you believe they were just one of the many acts of heroism from an unstoppable black-silk-draped Victorian lady who lived just before the turn of the century?

Born in 1862, no one would have said that Mary Kingsley was born under a bright star. Her father and mother were only married a few days before she was born. Afterward, her parents seemed to fade into the background of her life: Her mother was quite sick and her father, a doctor, traveled often and was rarely home. Mary led a lonely life in a house of servants and was not sent to school—but she desperately wanted to learn. At an early age, Mary needed to step into the role that her mother should have played. She ran the household, managed the servants, raised her little brother, and cared for her sick mother. Between all of these responsibilities, Mary never lost sight of her love of learning—which led her to learn German, Syrian, Latin, Arabic, and chemistry. But perhaps the books that determined the course of her life were those about famous explorers: They traveled throughout the wide world, engaging in exciting adventures that most could only dream about. For Mary, these adventures were even more removed, since as a Victorian woman, she would hardly be allowed to scale the heights of Everest or stumble about a dark jungle. Plus, Mary was desperately needed to run the family home. While Mary continued to study on her own, there seemed to be little light along her dark and lonely path.

Then Everything Changed

Both of her parents passed away in 1892. Her brother was already into his 20s, and needed no support. Suddenly, Mary found herself completely free to follow her dreams of exploration. She sent out letters to tell others about herself and to obtain advice about traveling, but many respondents attempted to put her off. Every letter sent was a risk, every piece of disheartening advice like a shock of icy water. Kingsley, however, learned from these missives, and instead of letting them get her down, she read them carefully to get a stronger picture of what her aims would entail. Kingsley sailed for West Africa in 1893—and began to follow her dreams of exploration. She studied the religions of Africa and collected specimens for the British Museum. Mary accomplished what no one else had: She became the first European—man or woman—to visit Gabon and certain parts of the Congo. She became well-known for her courage, resilience, and unbending determination to explore. Her adventures were stunning: She climbed an active volcano, collected strange creatures for the museum, and was one of the first Europeans to set eyes on a gorilla. She lived with cannibals and ate pythons. Perhaps more importantly, Mary wrote two books that opened a whole new world to those who had no hope of travel. In these texts, Mary's attractive, witty style not only laid bare the soul of Africa, but revealed the people there in 3D—she defied the common African stereotypes of the day to show that the African peoples were multifaceted and complex, with rich cultures and traditions. Kingsley learned from each experience and used her insight to help her remain unstoppable in the face of sexism, penury, jungle dangers, and river terrors.

Passion Play

How often will you fail before you realize your dreams? It all depends on you. You may realize that your initial goal was not really what you wanted. This may take a significant amount of time. It is important to not give up, though. Sometimes, the most important goal you can create for yourself is to find what your purpose or goal is. Your life is a journey, and you will find that you will walk down many different paths before you find the best way forward. No one else can judge your success.

When I first realized that companies were hiring people instead of positions, it completely changed how I approached my dreams. I always wanted to run my own business, but I had been going about it in the wrong way. I saw that I needed to create my own brand in order to really succeed. I also caught the tech bug. The amazing potential that exists in advanced technologies is astounding, but its benefits seem to be limited to very few people. I wanted to change that—make the world a better place by opening up the doors to technology to billions, not just the select few. In order to do that, though, I needed a platform. This was a bit of a problem. No one knew who I was. I did not have a technology degree. I had no CXO connections in the tech world. So I did the only thing I could think of: I began to write.

As any writer can tell you, the publishing world is brutal. I felt like I was on a perpetual rejection wheel. I kept pitching and trying to get my ideas about the intersection of man and technology in front of more eyes. Finally, after much rejection, I finally got in: *WIRED* magazine picked up some of my work. Suddenly, I had a platform. Other publications began to see value in my ideas, and I began to get noticed. My work was not only being published, but companies were asking me to speak about my ideas. As I mentioned earlier, I have struggled with public speaking. The idea of being in front of a crowd of people terrified me. But I knew that I needed to face this challenge. Getting up in front of that group for the first time was an exercise in sheer terror. But it taught me an incredible lesson: I had a powerful, more intimate impact on many more people all at the same time. Since my audience could see and hear me, the connections they made with my ideas were stronger than I expected. They saw "Scott, the man who is going to help me see what my future will look like." Being in front of a real audience also helped me realize how to communicate my ideas more effectively. It was a shocking experience, but it was only the first step. Soon, other opportunities became available, but I wanted more. I took another risk: I began to proactively seek out speaking engagements. Sometimes I needed to pay for everything, including the air fare, lodging, and even conference fees. You may think that I was crazy, and perhaps I was a little insane, but I was so motivated by what I had learned from my earlier risks that I knew it was something I should do. It began to pay off in fantastic ways, such as larger speaking engagements (I was voted into the Top 25 Speakers in the World at Speaker.com, served as part of the IoT panel at the United Nations, ITU at Budapest, and have spoken on TEDx Talk), greater contacts (I am now an IBM IoT Futurist, a board member of the Independent Oracle Users Group, and have been building relationships in Asia, Europe, the Middle East, and South America), and numerous awards. I was excited to finally be accomplishing my dreams–then I realized what my next big step had to be.

Your story of success is just beginning. Perseverance is an important tool that every successful person has in their toolbox. But how do you know when your risks are paying off? Can you recognize when your risks are moving you closer to your goals? I think you can—and the next chapter will highlight some ways you can verify the outcomes of your risks.

9 Verify and Magnify Your Success

Trust, but verify.

—Ronald Reagan, 40th president of the United States

Periodically Check to See If You Are Meeting Goals and Stretching Yourself to Achieve Success

What is real success? Is it having a lot of money or being famous? If that was the case, then people who were born to wealthy parents would be natural successes. That would also mean that teachers, caregivers, police officers, and many other people would never be considered successes. Money and fame can be the by-products of achieving your goals, but they are not the measuring rods of success. I would like to emphasize this point. It is an unfortunate fact that many young people believe that money and fame are the most important things in the world. Many of the individuals profiled in this book are extremely wealthy and famous, but not because I believe that only wealth and fame make you a success. These people obtained wealth and fame by achieving their goals. I believe that your own personal success is achieved when you attain your goals and personal growth. The media does not often write in great detail about a teacher who helps disadvantaged students overcome their challenges or a police officer who counsels high school students to stay in school. These stories are out there, but they tend to be included in articles with only some insight on a particular aspect of the person's success; their entire life is not laid before you like that of the leader of a nation or a pop star. You will be disappointed if you believe that money and fame equal success. Here are a few facts. The first is that most of us will never be extremely rich or famous. Credit Suisse showed that the top 1% of the wealthiest people in the world own more wealth than the remaining 99%. A short piece in *The Atlantic* noted that mathematician Samuel Arbesman actually attempted to calculate the number of famous people in the entire world. What was his stunning conclusion? Only 0.0086% (much less than 1%) of the people in the world can be considered famous. In an earlier chapter, I also showed that modern fame is ephemeral.

Success means attaining your goal. Success also means attaining your own personal growth. Now that we have examined goals and how to develop them, risks, and insights, let's focus on how to verify our success. How do you know that you have accomplished something? How can you determine if your risk has paid off?

In an article for *Harvard Business Review*, Michael J. Mauboussin dissected how companies evaluate success and how these methods of verification actually may not be delivering useful insights. Mauboussin used Michael Lewis's *Moneyball* as an example, and discussed how the Oakland Athletics' baseball team was able to find so many excellent players by completely revising the way talent scouts evaluated individual players. He noted that scouts were looking at things like power hitting and running ability, but what the team really needed was a player who could get on base often. This insight was garnered from a significant amount of data, so although it went against some of the scouts' gut instincts, the team decided to utilize this approach. Once the scouts began identifying these types of players—and they were not always the power hitters or the fastest men on the field—they were able to assemble a winning bench.

The important takeaway from this piece is that you must be sure that you are correctly evaluating and verifying the outcomes of your risks. If, for example, your business fails but you learned important lessons that will help you begin again, then you have experienced some success in the form of personal growth. Personal growth is what helps you mature and be able to manage the more difficult times during your journey to success. If you launch your business and it is relatively stable, then your goal of beginning a business has been reached. Simple.

The outcome of your uncomfortable changes and risks will be different based on your goals. For example, a family that adopts a disabled child would never consider the same benchmarks of success as those of a businessman. They would see success as being able to provide a loving home environment that enables that child to reach the height of their potential. When that child graduates from high school, that would be one way to verify their success. Another way to verify their success would be through the happy home life they all experience. Success in business is another matter. You can put hard numbers on things like increased revenue, new opportunities, and more employees.

We have now moved to the fifth part of Strive.

S—Set a goal.

T—Think about how to get there and plan for success.

R—Risk: Embrace it, expect it.

I—Insights, or what did you learn from your uncomfortable change or risk?

V—Verify progress.

E—Enhance yourself, mentally and physically, with safe biohacking.

Verify

There are two key ways to verify success. The first is through insights and personal growth. The second is through actual quantification.

When you embrace risk and uncomfortable change, you will experience some failure. You may try to get a position at a certain company, but not even be asked to interview. Or you might want to become a pilot but find that you cannot stomach the takeoffs or landings. In these situations, the insight or personal growth you have experienced becomes the verification of your progress to real success. What did you learn from the experience? Do you understand yourself better? Do you understand your goals better?

Personal Growth

Insights and personal growth can happen in any pursuit. It is very common to achieve them when you are pursuing goals that directly involve helping others. Parents cannot use actual data to quantify their success with their children (trust me, it doesn't work). The ultimate goal of any parent is to have their child become an independent, productive member of society. It is not always clear if a child needs extra help in a certain area or is just relying on the parents to do everything for them. However, as parents make mistakes and take risks, they eventually begin to understand themselves and their children better. This allows them to make more informed decisions and leads to greater success. Goals that are hard to quantify are those that are a little fuzzy to begin with: To become a better dad, to understand yourself more deeply, or to become more engaged with the people around you.

Even in the midst of your struggles and risk-taking, you may find that personal growth is happening in ways you did not imagine. This has happened to me on more than one occasion. For example, while I was struggling with finding the right job and trying to support my growing family, I decided to stretch myself and accept a leadership position at my local church. There, I was asked if I would mentor a man who was struggling in his own personal life. At first, I balked. How could I mentor someone else? I felt like I had reached the end of my own rope. I had merely tied a knot and was hanging on. I eventually agreed, even though I was wondering just what kind of impact I could possibly have. Discussing how to manage the struggles in life seemed to be outside my expertise.

But Then the Impossible Happened

I would meet with this man regularly. He was in despair over his marriage situation. We talked a lot and sometimes I felt like he could see that I was struggling as much as he was—if not more. However, not only did he begin to improve over the course of a year, but I actually saw his healing take place. Eventually, he was able to come to grips with his challenges and began to realize real transformation in his life. Watching this man heal was a strong point of personal growth for me. It made me understand that I did not need to be perfect to help other people. God does the heavy work. I simply needed to obey and show up. You do not need to be perfect, either. By taking risks, you can realize tremendous personal growth. But you must get outside your comfort zone.

Quantification of Outcomes

Another way to verify success is through actual quantification. It will be obvious that there are some goals that lend themselves more easily to quantification than others. For example, if your goal is to start your own business, and you do it, you can track your progress such as a successful business launch as well as financial, customer acquisition, and customer satisfaction/retention metrics. A list of key performance indicators (KPIs) like this can help you see your progress, and I highly encourage you to develop some goals that are easily quantifiable to help you move along your path to success. For example, instead of simply stating a goal of "getting into med school," include all the steps that would go along with it: Getting information from the different schools, filling in forms, writing essays, and sending all of the material before the deadline. Getting into med school is only the beginning, so your goal has to be broadened to include grades in med school, successful internship, passing the medical board, becoming a licensed doctor, and starting your practice. Quantifiable goals can be encouraging because they help you easily see yourself progressing.

Another way to quantify success is by using the many devices, apps, and programs we have at our disposal. For example, if you have a fitness goal, you could take advantage of an activity tracker like a Fitbit or Garmin. These would allow you to put a number on your goal and allow you to easily measure how close you are to reaching it. These types of devices can track an array of data, such as your heart rate, metabolic rate, body fat composition, and step count. What if your goal is to reduce the amount of stress in your life? It is not always easy to identify exactly the things that trouble us. For example, a 2014 study performed at Penn State showed that many people actually felt more stressed at home than they did at work, debunking the common fallacy that home was a safe haven from the tyranny of the workplace. New smart devices and wearables can determine your emotional state through various biometric markers, allowing you to get insights into the types of activities or kinds of people that impact your mental well-being. With watchOS 3, Apple introduced a new Breathe app with the goal of helping you to relax by focusing on your breathing. Garmin Vivosmart 3, using heart rate variability, tracks your heart and presents a stress level score throughout the day. If it's high, you can kick off a guided breathing exercise to recenter yourself. Touchpoints Basic promises to zap your stress in 30 seconds to help you think clearly and become calmer. It harnesses neuroscience technology to restore your homeostatic nervous system function by sending alternating vibrations that aim to alter the body's fight, flight, or freeze response to stress and anxiety. If you find that running a small business leaves little time to crunch the numbers, small business accounting programs like Xero, Wave, and FreshBooks can help you keep an eye on the bottom line to help you understand your financial progress.

Verifying your success is not very difficult. After you check your progress, you might find that you would like to accomplish more, or you believe that your risks should have had a greater return, but didn't. While every person's journey to success will be different, there is something you can do to move yourself into a stronger position to enjoy a greater audience and broader impact. However, before I discuss a way to enhance your success, I would like to cover an insidious practice that can prevent you from achieving it: Coasting.

Are You Coasting?

We've all done it. After a win, we tend to coast. As things get comfortable and routine, we coast. As long as someone else is taking care of everything, we coast. Coasting involves simply letting life go by without embracing any challenges. Coasting can delay, and even destroy, your ultimate success.

Perhaps the king of coasters was, in fact, a real king. Commodus (161–192 AD) ruled the Roman Empire after the death of his very famous father, Marcus Aurelius, the philosopher-king who was well loved by his people. Aurelius made a point out of leading an exemplary lifestyle, set a powerful example for others, and ruled in a strong, effective manner. There is little doubt that he hoped Commodus would follow in his footsteps.

Commodus did not follow in his father's footsteps. Instead, he left the path entirely.

Commodus had an excellent education, with a stable of tutors that attempted to shape the young man's intellect and character. Commodus was cared for by Galen, the great Greek physician who had a powerful influence on the study of medicine and philosophy. As the 17th emperor of the vast Roman Empire, Commodus even ruled jointly with Aurelius for a few years, enjoying the guidance of his wise father and counselors.

All seemed well until Marcus Aurelius died in 180 AD.

At 19, Commodus found himself in charge of the mightiest, most extensive empire the world had seen up until that point. In a strange about-face, Commodus decided to stop fighting to gain the disputed territories so coveted by Aurelius and instead made a peace treaty. He returned to Rome and there put down the first of several conspiracies against him. After this success, he did begin to govern somewhat by devaluing the currency. However, Commodus then proceeded to place the government in the hands of others while he indulged his every whim. He did not do much with his power—although there was much to do. The empire was recovering from the grip of the Antonine Plague that had officially ended in 180 but which had claimed the lives of over five million people. It had also significantly reduced the number of men who were qualified to become senators to help guide the policy of the empire. Such a vast domain required the guidance of a strong, wise ruler to not only fend off outside incursions, but to also provide the glue to keep the elite class from descending into violent conspiracies.

Instead of overseeing the problems of his empire, Commodus played sports and practiced fighting, and it was rumored he spent time with chariot racing. He would even sometimes appear as a gladiator at the games—and demand payment for his appearance. It should be understood that while gladiators in the American conscience are revered warriors, to the Romans, they were less than slaves. The shock of seeing an emperor appear in gladiatorial combat would be the equivalent of seeing a sitting president on the street corner begging for loose change. Commodus would dress as the mythical Hercules and "fight" all sorts of men and beasts; one of his inscriptions claimed that he killed over 12,000 men. His cruelty knew no bounds: He once heard that there was a gladiator who killed a lion from his chariot. Inflamed by jealousy over the man's prowess, Commodus had him executed. He spent enormous amounts of time with the members of his harem, rumored to be over 600 strong.

Although it is true that most of what we know about Commodus comes from sources written after his reign, generally by those who held him in an unfavorable light, there is not much argument that Commodus was never considered one of the great emperors. Commodus's lack of interest in government allowed corruption to become rampant, spilling over into every part of the machinery of the empire. For example, he was assassinated through a conspiracy involving a member of the Praetorian Guard, elite soldiers who were sworn to protect the emperor. Members of the Guard then auctioned off the position of emperor of Rome shortly after his demise. Commodus's successor, Septimus Severus, found himself embroiled in overwhelming difficulties at home and abroad.

Commodus shows us that coasting is human nature. But it can also slow or prevent you from attaining your goals. How do you know you are coasting or just taking full advantage of the outcome of one of your risks? The answer is not straightforward.

One way to tell that you are coasting is that you are spending inordinate amounts of time surfing the web, watching TV, or just hanging out. It's not that these things are bad in themselves (we all need a break), but if you find that you are spending increasing periods of time doing little or nothing, you may be coasting. The same could be true in your professional life. Sometimes, you will need to remain in a certain position for months or even years to really attain your long-term goals. For example, if you are an engineer fresh out of school, you may need to work at a technology company for several years before you really understand the business and the needs of customers. Only after you have gained a certain amount of experience will you be able to start your own venture. Other times, you may not be able to take a certain kind of risk because you have a higher priority. For example, a woman may want to attend business school full time, but needs to care for her children and aging mother at the same time. In this case, she can still work toward her goal of an MBA, but it will be through taking night and weekend courses over many years. In these types of situations, the people are not coasting, but rather accepting a delay of their goal attainment because of the need for experience or a higher priority.

But let's consider people who are really coasting. Let's say you obtained that first job. Over a five-year period, your goal was to get a position in management with more responsibilities. However, after working at the company for a few years, you had an increase in your salary and suddenly do not feel pressured to obtain that management position. You'll get to it ... someday. Coasting can also happen at home. Your wife may take care of the children, so you don't feel like you should give up your golf game to take them to the park on Saturday. You'll eventually take them somewhere, when the weather is not so nice ... someday. That's the problem with coasting. You feel comfortable, so you do not embrace uncomfortable change or risk to grow. Examine yourself: Are you coasting or still embracing uncomfortable change to achieve your dreams?

Magnify Your Success

If you have taken a hard look at your risks, outcomes, and insights, you will be able to verify if your actions have moved you closer to your goal. But by now, you may have realized that achieving goals depends on the kinds of goals you set, and not all of your goals are leading to the success you hoped for. Perhaps you have a small following on your YouTube channel or have been able to establish a limited presence in your local community.

You may need to do what I did: Become your own brand and platform. This can be applied to any kinds of goals or dreams, not just building a business. For example, actors and actresses basically become their own brand to "sell" their talents. Once they achieve a certain amount of success, they can become comfortable helping others launch themselves or even develop their own production companies. Building on your success by branding yourself and creating your own platform can powerfully magnify your voice and ideas. It can also help you attract other people who are interested in accomplishing the same types of goals—which will broaden your impact even more. In our social media age, becoming your own platform is not as hard as you may think.

The Magnifier

Who doesn't want to look good? Few of us would claim we have no desire to improve our appearance, and most would admit that they have many flaws. This broad audience—people who want to look better—is only eclipsed by one that is much greater—those who want to look better in 10 minutes or less.

Enter Michelle Phan, the Vietnamese-American phenomenon who has drawn rave reviews on YouTube and sits as queen of a more than $500 million empire. Phan's secret to success?

Personal Branding

Phan didn't start out with the idea of branding; her first thought was to help someone else out. After her father abandoned Phan and her mother, their lives became extremely difficult. Phan had a request from some friends about how she did her makeup, so she posted a short online tutorial to help them out. She thought only two people would see the video.

Four Thousand Did

It was then that Phan realized that people were hungry for more. She created many more tutorials, all designed to help women understand how to make the most out of their own features with makeup and cosmetics. Phan herself was more the product than the cosmetics—her casual, friendly explanations in every video provided quick insights for those trying to get "the look." Her positive, bouncy attitude was her springboard to success. Phan's YouTube following exploded. (She now boasts 8.9 million followers to date, with over one billion views, making her one of the top performers on YouTube.) She has since branched out to create Ipsy, which is built completely around her style and approach. Phan also understood early how important it was to connect with her fans and become a relatable "friend." She frequently uploaded videos with novel content, everything from how to get the look of Lady Gaga to how to prep your best face for the Chinese New Year. Phan addresses fan comments and actively solicits their feedback. Phan's brand has showboated other brands: When she posted a video featuring Dr. Pepper, it obtained 41 more times the views as the content on the soda maker's website, generating more than 304 times more "Likes."

Phan's journey of Strive is far from over. After taking an extended break from YouTube to travel the world for several months, she bought back Em Cosmetics, the failed beauty brand L'Oréal started with her, and relaunched it independently. She then transitioned out from Ipsy permanently to focus on Em Cosmetics as part of her new company, Divinium Labs, LLC.

The Platform Effect

Apple (iOS) has one. Amazon does, too. So does YouTube and Google (Android).

The Platform

Literally, platforms are raised structures that help you reach out physically. Platforms can raise workers up, so they can safely work on a structure. Platforms can also serve to hold up speakers, so more people can see and hear them. When you focus on achieving success, you will build a virtual platform that you—and others—can use to help you achieve goals.

In the *Harvard Business Review*, Mark Bonchek and Sangeet Paul Choudary identified three aspects of a successful platform: The toolbox, the magnet, and the matchmaker. In Bonchek's and Choudary's approach, the toolbox is what allows for others to connect with the platform and each other—much like how Wikipedia provides writers and editors to work on a page together to create and edit content. Their magnet refers to the pull of a particular platform. Every platform needs a lot of people to be involved in its creation and use, or otherwise it will fail. Boncheck and Choudary note that getting the word out about the platform is key: Social media and advertising are important. Finally, they highlight the need for a "matchmaker," or a middleman who can make connections between the various users of a platform to help create more value. Here, they identified how eBay assists buyers with finding products that may be interesting or helpful.

What would this look like for someone who does not directly work with computers and technology?

Network Effects

Your individual platform may vary from one designed for a computer system, but it will still be able to capitalize on something called the "network effect." The network effect is an important part of achieving success; it is defined as a phenomenon in which a product or service obtains more value as more people use it.

One example would be Adobe. The Acrobat Reader is given away for free, so anyone can download the software to read PDF files. Users want to do this because Acrobat's PDFs look the same on any device. Because PDFs have numerous other advantages, such as a small size compression and ability to preserve formatting, businesses prefer to use PDFs for important digital documents. In addition, many schools teach graphic designers how to create images with Photoshop and Illustrator. Adobe products are used widely in business and academia, so more people hear about them and use them.

The network effect can be seen in many other places, as well. For example, when Katy Perry releases a new song, it may be played in a few large cities. Through word-of-mouth, social media, and advertising, Perry's new song will be heard by others, who will, in turn recruit others to listen to the music.

Harnessing the power of the network effect means getting outside your comfort zone. This is because, although most people do enjoy interacting with others, the network effect involves reaching out to people who may be very different from you. This can be seen in the various ways that influencers like Michelle Phan reach out to others; they may be showing how to do something or answering a question, but they conduct themselves in a way that lets others see them as genuine. Letting others understand your motivation to achieve your goal is key to success. However, if you are naturally shy or a private person, it can be extremely challenging to do this. Building a platform will involve incorporating the principles of Strive.

Now What?

Once I began to draw more interest in my ideas and began speaking more, I realized that I absolutely needed to branch out. As one person, I could certainly have an impact by only writing and speaking. However, I found that there were many others like me with amazing, useful ideas—but no global platform to make them come to life.

This was why I began my company, Amyx+, and eventually created my VC fund, Amyx Ventures. I have the know-how, experience, and background that can move these individuals into the places they need to go. I not only understand the business environment, but I have a talent for quickly identifying trends— a boon for anyone in the tech business. Amyx+ became an innovation lab for IoT and wearable concepts, where we not only helped tech-savvy individuals and businesses fully realize and prototype their ideas, but we also helped them connect with the right manufacturers and partners to bring their dreams to life.

I began Amyx+ several years ago to help companies bring their ideas to market. Since its launch, I am very proud to say that the company has started many great ideas on their way. We've also been enjoying a significant amount of attention from groups that award innovation in technology. But more importantly, we are bringing about real change for people. This is not to say that I always saw a clear way forward. I realized that I wanted to be able to promote companies that I felt would have a real impact on the world. That was when I started Amyx Ventures, my own VC fund that is now making inroads in nations in Asia, Europe, the Middle East, and South America to help bring exponential technologies, job creation, and a better life to those regions that are seeking to transform their nations.

I hope that you are embracing risk and uncomfortable change in your life in order to pursue yours dreams. However, I would be remiss if I did not add that there is one more very important aspect of Strive that is necessary for real success: Taking care of yourself. How can you persevere if you are on the bench for stress-related illnesses? How can you enjoy your success if you can't get out of bed in the morning? In the next chapter, we will look at how Strivers can take care of themselves and even practice some safe "biohacking" to move themselves further along their paths to success.

10 Enhance Yourself

The first wealth is health.

—Ralph Waldo Emerson, American transcendentalist

Success Without Self-Care Is Failure

Bloated

That's what I thought about myself one day when I happened to come across a recent photo of myself. I stared at the picture for a long time. A juicy steak, an extra slice of cheesecake—these kinds of things tasted so good going down, but when I saw myself, I realized that my eating habits were wrecking my body. I knew I wasn't young anymore, but I didn't realize that I would look so unhealthy when I hit my 30s. I didn't just look sickly, either. I didn't feel well, and my physical health was impacting my attitude. I decided that I needed to do something immediately, so after some discussion with my wife, we decided to go raw vegetarian.

Cold Turkey

I didn't allow myself any transition foods or cut myself some slack. Every day I chowed down on bags of sliced raw vegetables like beets, carrots, and tomatoes. Needless to say, this had an immediate effect on my digestive system. (Let's just say I felt sorry for my coworkers.) However, the amazing thing about changing my diet so radically was that I looked and felt better. It was as if the years had melted away. My flagging energy gradually returned, and I found that I could manage my moods better. My skin cleared up and I looked younger. I stayed on that diet for about three years, and then switched to one that incorporated a wider variety of foods. Now, I eat carefully considered portions of food that give me the energy I need to accomplish my goals and make me feel good. I do not want to tell anyone to go meat-free. Every person is different, and some people really should have animal products in their diet to enjoy good health. But I do believe that cutting out the fatty junk foods is a key component of a good diet—and ultimately, your continued success. You cannot really achieve your dreams if you do not take care of your body and mind. Your personal well-being underpins real, lasting success. How strong of a business can you build if you are always sick in bed? How many connections can you make if you are too tired to go to events?

Since I am heavily involved with technology and business, I have come across many people who are attempting to enjoy greater success by either unsafely modifying their bodies through technology or by ingesting substances. The term "biohacking" usually refers to altering the body through gene modification, but it has also been used more loosely to refer to the modification of the body through the utilization of science and technology.

Leveraging technology to increase your reach and help achieve your goals is beneficial. There are now many devices and apps on the market that can help you track your personal biometrics and understand how your body is responding to your activity or your environment. On my own path to success, I found that I needed to take care of my body. However, I also found many people who were trying to obtain success through very unhealthy means. Damaging your body to achieve goals is pointless.

We have now moved to the final part of Strive.

S—Set a goal.

T—Think about how to get there and plan for success.

R—Risk: Embrace it, expect it.

I—Insights, or what did you learn from your uncomfortable change or risk?

V—Verify progress.

E—Enhance yourself, mentally and physically, with safe biohacking.

My first foray into biohacking, changing my diet to include fresh, raw organic vegetables, was eye-opening: I just felt incredible. I didn't need stimulants to stay awake or chemical enhancements to boost my creativity. I was at the top of my game, and I have not slowed down since. But I am not only watching my diet. I also believe in taking care of every part of my well-being. However, it is common for people to want to take the shortcut to success. In the next few sections, I hope I can persuade you that the shortcut is actually anything but a shortcut, and the power of technology can help you enjoy physical and mental well-being—if used correctly.

Hacking the Body—By Any Means?

There are dangers in anecdotal evidence, especially when it comes to biohacking the human body. Take, for example, Thomas Hariot. Hariot was a vital part of Sir Walter Raleigh's expedition to Roanoke Island in 1585, as he not only had a strong understanding of navigation and mathematics, but spoke Algonquin, a Native Indian language. Hariot was a dedicated scholar (among many other accomplishments, he created two maps of the moon and developed a treatise on navigation) and a convincing storyteller, becoming the spokesman for an incredible plant that was cultivated by the Native Americans. He wrote that this marvelous plant "openeth all the pores and passages whereby their bodies are notably preserved in health and know not many grievous diseases, wherewithal we in England are often times afflicted." Many British subjects were able to obtain this amazing remedy and quickly implemented it into their daily health regime. The herbal remedy became popular all over the world, and to this day, large portions of the population still partake of it—despite the fact that we have scientifically proven that it causes multiple types of cancer, COPD, and enormously increases your chances of dying early. The Indians referred to it as uppowoc, but it is better known by its English name: Tobacco.

Although most health-conscious people these days would not willingly smoke tobacco, they do other things that may be just as damaging to their long-term performance based on anecdotal evidence. In order to strive and achieve your goals, you must understand that taking care of your physical and mental health are key parts of that success. You will not enjoy a better life if your creativity and productivity rely on unnatural chemical stimulation.

We naturally understand that if we want to succeed, we need to have energy, creativity, and stamina. We also know that a clear mind and strong body are important. How you go about achieving those aspects of your success is critical—there are no shortcuts to victory. The human body is an incredibly complex machine. Despite advances in technology and medicine, though, there are still many things about the body that we do not understand. One of these things is the human brain. For example, mankind has successfully used different methods for pain control throughout the generations. Modern anesthesia is a miracle of science. However, we have no idea how it works in the brain.

Many aspects of the brain are shrouded in mystery, but this is not because researchers have failed to take an interest. The National Institutes of Health (U.S.) spent over $4.5 billion in 2014 on brain research. The Chinese have implemented their Five-Year Plan, which includes a strong focus on brain research that will tap a science fund that is worth 2.5% of China's GDP (at about $11 trillion, a staggering $275 billion). In 2013, the Europeans invested 500 million euros on brain research. Yet for all that hard cold cash, we still have much to learn. For example, we still do not have any idea about how information is encoded, how the firing of neurons actually impacts your behavior, how consciousness works, how we perceive things, and, of course, how to address those very thorny questions dealing with issues like free will and personality. This, of course, doesn't mean that we should not keep trying to understand the brain, but rather that we should be cautious when someone begins to tinker with the delicate chemistry of the body's most important organ.

Biohacking

Although increasing performance can help you reach success, there are some approaches that may seem useful but are actually self-defeating. One of these alarming trends is microdosing.

Microdosing refers to taking a small amount of a drug to gain an enhanced performance. Like athletes who take steroids, these users claim to experience a physical improvement. Besides the obvious ethical issues of taking drugs (LSD, after all, is still illegal), there are other problems with this type of hacking. For example, although we may not know much about the brain, we have much solid research evidence to show that LSD definitely causes damage to it. In addition, LSD causes hallucinogen-persisting perception disorder (HPPD); "flashbacks" can occur for years after initial use of the drug, and these are basically recurrences of the effects of the drug even though it is not being used. Just imagine standing in front of possible investors when you suddenly have a flashback ... all of your hard work and passion would go up in smoke.

Nootropics are another area where the striver should beware. Nootropics can refer to any type of chemical that may be used to enhance cognitive performance. They can include Chinese medicine, like ginseng for energy, as well as prescription-based medicines like Adderall, which is typically prescribed for those who suffer from ADHD, and DHA (docosahexaenoic acid), an omega-3 fatty acid that is a main structural part of the human brain. Ginseng and DHA are frequently sold in the United States as supplements and have been designated as GRAS (Generally Recognized As Safe), but it is difficult to quantify their impact on the human body. Some studies show positive effects and others show little to no effect. In addition, knowing how much of these types of substances to take is difficult to determine. If you are interested in taking supplements, you should consult a medical professional. The first concern is, of course, efficacy, but even GRAS supplements can have interactions with each other or other drugs you may be taking. For example, fish oil supplements have been found to negate the efficacy of certain cancer drugs. Ginseng can increase the chance of bleeding when taken in conjunction with aspirin. Taking prescription drugs when you do not have a condition that requires treatment is irresponsible. The whole point of Strive is to embrace uncomfortable change and risk with a clear, healthy mind. It is not possible to understand all the effects of a prescription drug on the normal human body, which is why these drugs are offered only through consultation with a doctor. It can be extremely dangerous to take prescription drugs in order to enhance yourself. I strongly discourage it. The side effects of prescription drugs can be traumatic. For example, several studies highlighted the fact that there has been a tremendous spike in the number of serious ER visits by users of ADHD prescriptions. The users of these prescription drugs were taking them to enhance cognitive performance (although, it should be noted that it seems few people actually improved their grades or abilities by taking them), but ended up with cardiac-related issues. Are you dying to achieve success?

Ingesting chemicals is not the only unsafe and self-defeating practice. There are also individuals who attempt to go outside the regulatory walls of institutions to play Dr. Frankenstein. The so-called "garage biology movement" involves setting up a DIY lab in your home or garage and then attempting to enhance the body through the utilization of science or technology. It sounds great—a community of DIYers who are trying to push the boundaries of the human body.

Or Maybe Not

Scientists are already creating artificial limbs or organs to help those who suffer from amputations or other challenges. We will, eventually, be able to augment our bodies safely with technology, but like all science that directly affects the human body, its development must be carefully regulated to keep the individual and society safe. Since the body is complex, tinkering with it can have unknown consequences, even in areas not immediately associated with the enhancement. The ethics behind biohacking are quite serious, and I am sure you can come up with your own concerns. Besides the obvious questions about what makes us human and the possibility of uploading the consciousness to a computer, there are privacy concerns that take center stage. Unfortunately, many of these concerns are downplayed by both individuals and businesses alike. In 2015, I developed a short guide, *The Data Privacy Playbook for Wearables and the IoT,* that briefly addressed some privacy issues and ethical considerations in relation to the development of wearables. In that guide, I highlighted numerous issues that must be addressed about how wearables can be effectively brought to market and used to help people advance—safely and with a concern for privacy. Would you want your neighbor creating and utilizing devices that allow him to know your personal biometric information throughout the day? Would you want to wake up one morning to find that your bike helmet has been replaced by one that can remotely control your movements, like the one created by Allan Pan? The simplest of wearable devices are can be extremely controversial. Remember how Americans created the new vocabulary word "Glasshole"? Utilizing technology must be done in a safe and effective manner. (Incidentally, there is a noticeable lack of medical professionals in the garage biology movement.)

Future You

There is incredible technology out there that is currently being developed in labs across the world, both commercially and academically. This technology is more amazing than a fitness tracker and it will soon become a part of your daily life. Right now, you have access to apps and wearables that can help you track your moods, heart rate, oxygen levels, footsteps, and location. But there will be many other safe extensions for you to use. For example, Ekso Bionics' Human Universal Load Carrier (HULC) is an exoskeleton that augments the power of the human body so one can lift amazing amounts of weight. Motorola has snagged the patent for an electronic throat device that allows you to issue voice commands to a computer from wherever you are. Designers and scientists are turning their attention to smart fabrics, e-textiles, and graphene to create eye-catching, utilitarian clothing that can let you unobtrusively protect yourself from harsh cold or hot environments and understand and amplify your mood while still looking great. All of these devices will become part of your tomorrow—after they have been vetted to ensure their safety. I believe in taking risks, but strivers must take smart risks. Any technology must be carefully evaluated for its impact on the individual and the others around them.

Eventually, we may (safely) move beyond simply augmenting our abilities with technology to completely becoming more than human. The transhumanism movement is dedicated to making technologies broadly available to people and enhancing the human mind and body far beyond their current capacity. Man has always dreamed of eternal life, and transhumanists believe that technology will eventually take us there. Perhaps the most audacious member of the transhumanist movement is a man who believes that computers will grant us eternal life. Russian billionaire, Dmitry Itskov, sees the name of his project (2045) as the deadline for his life's work. Itskov believes that he can figure out a way to upload the human mind into a computer, resulting in a sort of "eternal life" for the consciousness. Besides the obvious questions, such as "Should we live forever?" "Who gets to do it?" and, of course, "Who pays for it?" the more pressing question is, "Is it possible?"

Perhaps

Ideas of becoming superhuman, like transhumanism, or living forever in a robotic body, like the 2045 project, are interesting and exciting. They open up whole new worlds for us. They encourage us to pursue new avenues of growth that can benefit all mankind. However, before you begin to sign up to put your brain on a computer, please consider that many of these ideas are based on an expected desired growth rate in the area of technology. The problem is that while we are beginning to grow artificial limbs, we do not have artificial bodies. Any medical professional will be able to tell you that every aspect of the human system needs to be perfect in order to work in concert with the rest of the body – no mean feat. This is part of the problem with organ donations. Some people may get a life-saving organ transplant, but the body itself may reject it. Creating an entire artificial body may be in our future, but for your success, I would encourage you to take care of what you have right now. The technology we have now is more than sufficient to help you on your journey to success. As a matter of fact, you can achieve much of your success by standing on some basic research about the human body.

Busy = Better?

You have probably seen those kinds of commercials. Little Caesar's has one where the "busy people" are all eating lunch at their desks at the office. KFC has Norm McDonald on the phone, stamping documents, and typing all at the same time. Even Weight Watchers has a commercial where a busy professional is working and getting fed by an assistant. All of these images present busyness as a natural and normal part of life—something expected.

Are you always busy? Is it hard to relax or find the time to meet up with friends or read a book? Our modern society tells us that we must be busy: If you are not busy, you are lazy or not managing your time well. After all, we all get the same 24 hours in a day. What you do with them ultimately determines your overall success. But what is busyness? How is it really affecting our lives? Is being busy the same as being productive?

Part of striving to achieve your goals involves uncomfortable change, so what I am going to include in this section may make you very uncomfortable. This is because it goes against everything you see on TV, everything you see in the media, everything you read about in magazines, and everything you hear from the people around you.

Busyness does not equal productivity.

In a piece in *Harvard Business Review*, Sarah Green Carmichael noted that overwork actually limits productivity. She found that this is a business insight that was first noticed during the heyday of manufacturing. In the 1800s, the average workweek was more than 70 hours; most workers were employed in terrible conditions doing back-breaking labor. However, when employers were forced to change the workday to a maximum of eight hours, they were shocked to see that productivity soared. This fact is borne out by OECD data, which shows that Mexico, which has the world's longest average workweek, is at the bottom when it comes to worker productivity. On the opposite

end, Germany and the Netherlands have the shortest average
workweeks, but enjoy the highest productivity per worker. Being
too busy can keep you from greater productivity and decrease
your chances of achieving your goals. Why?

Busyness typically involves trying to manage multiple projects
or activities at the same time. Physically, this is impossible. René
Marois and his team from Vanderbilt University used MRIs
to show that a bottleneck occurs in the brain when you try to
multitask, so your brain cannot focus on two different tasks
at exactly the same time. Instead, your mind switches quickly
from one thought to another and then back again. You are not
really working on two projects at the same time. You are simply
switching your attention. This switching is a productivity killer.

David Meyer, a professor at the University of Michigan's
Cognition and Perception Program in the Psychology
Department, found that your productivity drops when you
begin switching between tasks to finish them. On average, he
found a 25% drop in the productivity for *both* tasks. Imagine that
it takes you one hour to finish your slides for a presentation and
another hour to create charts and graphs. By switching between
these two tasks, you will have wasted a total of 30 minutes. Now
multiply that number by the times you are interrupted with
e-mails, meetings, phone calls, and chats with coworkers, and you
may be wasting hours every day.

Researcher Jennifer Ackerman found that many people are
at their most productive in the first few hours after they wake
up—between two and four hours, specifically. But if we are
honest, we know that some people are night owls and others
are early risers—there's no one perfect strategy. This is where
self-quantification can help. By tracking your vital signs with apps

and commercially available smart devices, you can uncover your personal best times to approach tasks—or relax.

It's pretty clear that there are many unsafe things people do that they believe will enhance their success. There are, however, some safe approaches you can use to enhance your success.

Good Health—Do You Measure Up?

I am not a doctor. I don't even play one on TV. But I do believe there are some things that can underpin your success and even launch you toward greater accomplishments. I have an extremely busy schedule. I can speak in Saudi Arabia on Monday and be in Seoul the next day. In order to be able to maintain my stamina, I pay close attention to my body. The first and most important part of my routine is, of course, a healthy diet. You are what you eat. As I mentioned earlier, I have changed the way I eat to include more fresh organic fruits and vegetables. Your dietary needs will probably vary somewhat from mine, but dropping unhealthy fatty foods from your diet will likely pay off.

Physical exercise also plays an important role in your success. Not only does exercise help you control your weight, it can improve or eliminate certain health conditions, as well as boost your energy level and mood. There are many types of exercise, and you need to find out what kinds are especially beneficial to your lifestyle and health. Your best bet is to consult your physician to ensure that you are engaging in a really great exercise program. However, no matter how great an exercise program is, if you don't follow it, you won't benefit from it. Not all exercise is for every person. Running is beneficial, but you may find that running is too hard on your spine or joints. Yoga can aid in flexibility, but you may find that it does not help you reach your fitness goals. You may prefer kickboxing or Taekwondo to high intensity interval training (HIIT). Whatever program you choose, I recommend that you monitor your own progress through your biometrics in a journal. Just as you can monitor your biometric data to figure out what time of day is your personal best, monitoring and recording your vitals in response to your exercise program can show how you are progressing or if you have entered a danger zone. I am not particular to any device, app, or program. But there are many devices out there that can help you track your information and help you understand yourself better, as well as know when to see a doctor. Devices and apps should never be used for self-diagnosis (of a disease). They are only tools that can help you enhance your chances of success. For example, checking your heart rate shows if you have reached an ideal range. Understanding how many footsteps you have taken will allow you to push higher to achieve more. You should look at the data from all these devices and apps as Personal Empowerment Points. Each piece of data can help you understand yourself and allow you to increase your performance. They operate as a kind of Digital Currency of Happiness, where you find that sweet spot for your health, performance, and success.

Your Digital Currency of Happiness can be used beyond your fitness routine, too. When the FitBit was first launched, it was seen as a tool to help track exercise progress. But myriad devices like it can help us with so much more—we can see our blood glucose level after we eat or sleep, track our heart rate in various situations (such as when we meet someone new, our in-laws, or your boss), and measure certain other aspects of the human body after exercise, eating, sleeping, playing sports, working, watching TV, playing video games, and reading books.

Self-quantification, monitoring your personal biometrics in a journal to understand your health and well-being, puts power into your hands. Imagine the different kinds of decisions you would make about going to see the doctor. For example, say you don't feel well, so you wonder if you should set up an appointment. There are two possible approaches here. You could decide to wait until after next month's big sales meeting, since you have not been monitoring your personal biometrics. Or, if you are monitoring your biometric information, you find that your blood sugar has spiked dramatically and decide to make an appointment as soon as possible. In the first situation, you are basing your decision to see the doctor on an uninformed feeling. The second approach is based on knowing that there is something wrong inside you—and knowing can not only help you improve your performance, it could save your life.

Technology is enabling us to quantify, optimize, and accelerate our personal development without the need to depend on microdosing or any drugs. It's optimization through data analytics. Eventually, you will be able to partner your personal data with an AI personal assistant who can help you in understanding your health.

Boost Your Brainpower

Exercise helps you control your weight, improve or eliminate certain health conditions, boost your energy level and mental focus, and may even help you partially fend off some of the declines associated with old age. A recent study performed by the Centers for Disease Control showed that people who vigorously exercised had longer telomeres, a biological marker of aging. (Shorter telomeres are associated with aging.) Although this research is still in its early stages, you have probably already noticed that there are older people around you who enjoy exceptionally good health and mental clarity despite their advanced age.

You don't have to be a senior citizen to enjoy the brain-boost from exercise. Exercise strengthens your current mental acuity and willpower. Researchers at the University of British Columbia have shown that exercise actually increases the size of the hippocampus. Other studies have indicated that the prefrontal cortex and medial temporal cortex experience growth as well. The enhancement of the hippocampus has a direct effect on your ability to learn and remember what you learned. Exercise has also been shown to affect your attention span: Students who engaged in regular rigorous exercise were able to improve their focus in school. They were also able to better control themselves and retain what they learned.

Exercise has clear benefits that can help you on the road to success. But let's face it—sometimes we are simply too tired or don't feel like doing it. That is where willpower comes into play: Once you understand that a healthy lifestyle is part of your ultimate success, you will be more likely to pursue good health. Now imagine how you could know exactly when to exercise to obtain the maximum benefits to your body and mind—technology can give this to you. By tracking yourself through your health journal, you can obtain more powerful insights into your personal health and well-being.

Stress, Rest, and Your Brain

Silicon Valley types are burning the candle at both ends—but no one can keep up that pace forever. And no one should. If you are not convinced, consider the following. In Japan, death from overworking is so common that it has its own special term: Karōshi. In 2015, the number of claims of death from overwork were an astonishing 2,310. That number may even be higher since that is only counting families who have petitioned the government for compensation. (One estimate said that it is around 10,000 people a year.) A study by the Japanese government in 2016 found that approximately 20% of the working population was at risk of death from overwork. (A little perspective: There are about 66 million workers, making the total at-risk population a whopping 13.2 million people.) Many of those who suffer karōshi are in their 20s and 30s.

Your body is complex. When you are young, the occasional all-night cram session for chemistry or physics may not be a problem, but now imagine that you are cramming every single night for a "test" the next day—your job. The human body can only handle so much stress before it begins to break down—and sometimes, you won't even know it until real damage is done.

Huffington Post publisher Arianna Huffington is no stranger to challenges and understands first-hand how vital rest is to success. The high-powered entrepreneur was a hands-on person who worked diligently to see her dreams come true. However, she allowed one aspect of her life to completely lapse—sleep.

It Cost Her Dearly

In 2007, Huffington suffered from exhaustion, so much that she actually fell and broke her cheekbone. It was a wake-up call that she needed a good night's rest. Huffington wrote about not getting enough sleep in her book, *The Sleep Revolution*. She detailed the negative outcomes of not getting enough rest and provided recommendations for how to get a good night's sleep. Her new venture, health and wellness media start-up Thrive (no relation to Strive), is about helping people understand themselves and attain a good night's rest.

Scientists know certain aspects of sleep promote the overall health and wellness of an individual. Although there are disagreements over the optimum amount of sleep needed—and really, there will be no one correct answer since every person is unique—all research points to adequate amounts of rest, which is around eight hours a night for adults. For example, there are strong links between poor sleeping patterns and heart problems, diabetes, and obesity. It does not even take very long for poor sleeping patterns to affect health; in one case, it only took four days for health problems to appear in healthy people. Research has also shown that adequate levels of sleep can lessen chronic pain, improve your mood, make it easier to focus, improve your ability to retain memories, and help you lose weight.

Sleeping all night is a useful part of your plan for success, but napping can also be a part of it. In a study published in *Neurobiology of Learning and Memory,* researchers found that a nap during the day can ramp up your ability to remember fivefold. Napping, just like sleep, is vital to memory retention: The hippocampus (the same area affected negatively by constant stress) helps us save our memories, but it is a fragile area of the brain—lack of sleep has a tremendously negative effect on it. When you nap, your memories are placed into a long-term and more reliable storage area, the neocortex. The more you store after a rest, the more you will be able to recall when you require it. Sleeping and napping are vital to your success. You may want to track how many minutes you nap and sleep during the week to find out the optimum levels for you.

Meditation Can Rewire Your Brain—For Good

There's a reason that meditation is a part of the world's major religions: It offers the practitioner unique benefits. In our busy world, we rush from one project to another, one meeting to another, and one continent to another, but are we really accomplishing as much as we think?

Meditation, defined as a set of breathing exercises to help the mind reach calm and silence, can help lead to greater success. I discovered this when I was building technology start-ups. I was so stressed that I realized I needed to do something to help myself. I began to meditate and found that it boosted my feelings of well-being and allowed me to focus better on solving my problems. I continued to meditate even after the startup grew into a great success. It was eventually scooped up by a Fortune 500 company. Although I was asked to stay on with the new parent company, I decided that what I needed to do was to strike out on my own. I took a tremendous risk: I started my own tech company that created a robo-advisory product. Although robo-advisory is beginning to take off now, I was a bit too early to attract the kind of investment required to really succeed. I had eaten through all of our savings. I invested everything I had in that business. After three years, I was in agony: I was forced to let all my employees go. My family only had enough money to live on for two months—and nothing to show for all my efforts and investment. I thought I knew what I was doing, since I had accomplished a major merger and acquisition. But I still failed. I didn't trust myself. I second-guessed myself. I could not believe in myself. Meditation helped me during these tough times, and allowed me to see the larger picture that is my whole life, not merely professional success.

Researchers have shown that meditation offers many benefits. For example, one study showed that people who meditated regularly had a higher emotional intelligence (EI), less perceived stress, and fewer negative mental health issues than those who did not. A study in the *Social Science Journal* showed that students who meditated reported lower amounts of pain and did not need to engage in the use of tranquilizers to fall asleep. (Incidentally, meditation can be used for all kinds of people, even those who are not busy professionals. One study involved inmates at a correctional facility, and regular meditation reduced inmates' feelings of rage and the need to strike out at others, improved sleep, and increased feelings of well-being.)

Meditation can improve your life, and it is something you can do right now. The great thing about meditation is that anyone can do it and it offers everyone some benefits. For example, people who meditate generally feel less anxious than those that do not. This is because meditation has a physical effect on your brain and how it functions. Part of your brain, the medial prefrontal cortex, manages information about your daily experiences. When you are afraid, the medial prefrontal cortex is strongly affected because the neural pathway from the area of your brain where you feel fear is strongly connected to it. Meditation loosens this connection and allows you to more rationally perceive your experiences and environment.

Meditation can help you improve your creativity and memory. Have you ever felt like your creative tank was empty? Or how about those times when you just know you had a good idea yesterday but find that it has left the building today? You don't need to be a writer to understand "writer's block"; there are definitely versions of it in every profession. (Ever hear a speaker who suddenly pauses and fills in the awkward silence with "um"?) Meditation can help solve both of these problems. Dr. Catherine Kerr found that those who meditate have improved memory recall because they are able to adjust their brain waves (their sensory cortical alpha rhythms) to eliminate distractions. Meditation has been shown to improve memory, increase intelligence, increase feelings of compassion, decrease negative feelings, and improve sleep. Meditation is an aspect of Strive that can help you achieve your dreams.

Some Final Words

I would like to leave you with a few thoughts. Your success is in your hands, but it involves you reaching beyond yourself to embrace risk and change. Goal-setting, planning, carefully considering your path, and taking care of yourself can lead you to heights you have never imagined. If you would have told me 10 years ago that I would be the head of a venture capital fund and helping to bring about transformation in nations, I probably would have thought you were crazy. But here I am. I am healthier than I have ever been. I am spending more time with my family and doing the things that are important to me. I am reaching out and grabbing my dreams, and helping others do the same. I have found real success in my life through taking risks and embracing change. I know you can too.

> Day by day, what you choose, what you think, and what you do is who you become.
>
> *—Heraclitus, Greek philosopher*

EPILOGUE

Without a struggle, there can be no progress.
—Frederick Douglas, American author and abolitionist

Your Personal Journey to Success Will Be Entirely Unique

By now, you have probably realized that while there are many roads to success, there is only one personal path for you to follow to find your dreams. But what does it mean to really strive in your life? Are there any pitfalls on the way to success? What are the real metrics of success?

My own success is unbelievable because I suffered so many setbacks throughout my life. I was abandoned by my biological father and suffered the constant absence of my struggling mother. My mother's extended family refused to care for me. I was a stranger in a strange land who did not speak the language and could not understand the blind hatred of others. I was a foster child, seized by the state from my suffering mother, whose complete mental breakdown was a horror she would never recover from. I was moved from foster home to foster home, trying to find someone—anyone—who would believe in me. I found, and lost, the true love of parents who believed in me and a father who gave his all for my well-being. I suffered under the sheer rage of my youth, allowing it to poison my marriage and professional life. Poor posture and overwork led to the agony of a herniated disk. Unhealthy habits contributed to my poor health. I sank all my family's savings into businesses, only to see one nosedive no matter how hard I worked and another collapse in utter ruin.

But the principles of Strive have brought me to the success I enjoy today.

I did not need to go down a dark path where I let my circumstances or pessimistic feelings control me. I could have continued to blame others for my problems and feel sorry for myself, but that meant I would never find real freedom or success in my life. Instead, I chose to pursue healing and victory. In order to find those objectives, I needed to make difficult choices and embrace risk. I strove to beat the odds that are against children in foster care when I graduated from college, a member of the miniscule 6% to do so. I was able to open my heart to others, accepting a father's real love into my young but world-weary soul. I admitted that I needed help and saw a counselor, despite the incredible social stigma against it. I reached out to help others, even when I was not feeling good about myself. I humbled myself and admitted my failure to those closest to me, asking them to forgive me. I embraced risk in my personal and professional life. I have overcome my natural reticence about being around people and speaking in public. I have launched businesses—failed—and tried again. Now, I am effectively steering my own business through the waters of a global economy. I have successfully launched my own venture capital fund, and I am changing the world. I am an emotionally stronger man now than I was ten years ago. I am more physically and mentally fit, as well. I no longer see myself as subject to the whims of fate, but rather as a leader and helper to those who want a better life. The consummation of all my struggles, setbacks, and trials was the understanding that it is only through embracing uncomfortable change and risk that any real victory is achieved. It is true for me, and I believe it is true for you.

Should Success Be Measured Only by Money, Status, and Power?

"Show me the money!"

Remember that scene from *Jerry McGuire*? A desperate Jerry McGuire (Tom Cruise) is trying to convince Rod Tidwell (Cuba Gooding Jr.) to stay with him. Tidwell is only interested in the bottom line—a sports contract that will ensure his financial position and make him well known. This line has become the siren song of our modern life: Money and fame are what make us a success.

This could not be further from the truth.

Throughout this book, I have highlighted many people who have achieved success. Although most of them are very wealthy and powerful (like Oprah and Jeff Bezos), there are others (like Violet Jessup and Mary Kingsley) who did not attain great financial returns, but who are, nevertheless, tremendous successes. Personally, I do not believe success can be measured in terms of bank books or private islands. True success comes when you achieve your goals. Wealth and fame can be the by-products of your success, but they are not the sole indicators of your success.

One of the most important lessons I have learned on this journey is to question what we mean by success. Society hammers us with the idea that success should be measured by wealth, status, and power. But shouldn't we consider other metrics?

Economists measure usefulness or satisfaction with utility: Utility is defined as "the degree of removed discomfort or perceived satisfaction that an individual receives from an economic act." For example, let's say that you are driving down the highway and notice that your windshield wipers are no longer working well. Buying and replacing those wipers allows you to remove the discomfort of not being able to see through the windshield. Utility could be one useful way to measure success. Has a goal created something useful for you or other people? In what way was it useful? Perhaps your primary goal is to become a teacher. By achieving entrance into a teaching college, you have attained the first step on your journey. It is useful to you because getting into school allows you to study for the degree. It benefits others because you are working towards a profession that will profoundly impact the future of the children you teach.

In Chapter 10, I recommended using technology to help track your personal data to obtain insights into your physical health and well-being. Using a digital journal allows you to understand how you are progressing on your path to success. You can track the utility of your progress in a simple way: Record a "0" for no utility or a "1" for usefulness in your journal. You may want to record these values daily or weekly, depending on your goals. For example, if you went to class and finished your homework, then that would be a "1" because this exercise had value for achieving your goal. (If, however, you skipped class to play *StarCraft II* with your friends, you should record a "0," even if you advanced to a higher league.)

Psychologists measure satisfaction in a slightly different way: They try to ascertain their objectives by surveying people about their emotions and self-perceived wellness. This can also be a useful approach for measuring success. How has your goal (or your attempt to reach it) improved your satisfaction with your life? Has it helped others enjoy their lives or allowed them to achieve their goals? Measuring satisfaction in this way is subjective—and changeable. Some days, you may feel that your first few steps along your path to success were great and other days you may feel that they were not as wonderful as you hoped. Psychologists have developed a number of tools that can help you more accurately assess your position. You can actually measure your own satisfaction with clinically developed assessments that are available for free online, such as the Satisfaction With Life Scale (SWLS) and the Positive and Negative Affect Schedule (PANAS). These tests, and others, were developed to help evaluate individual satisfaction.

You can also track your own personal satisfaction ratings in your journal, but using a more complex approach than that for recording utility. You may want to start with a daily schedule of monitoring your satisfaction with your progress toward your goals. A simple scale (say, 1–5, with 5 being the most satisfied) can provide additional insights into your moods and sense of accomplishment. I also recommend including a few sentences describing why you feel the way you do. If you find that you are consistently scoring under 4, you may need to examine why you lack satisfaction with your progress toward your goals. What can you do to change it? Are you coasting or is there an obstacle that needs to be overcome?

Sometimes, these markers of utility and satisfaction can provide us with deeper insights into ourselves. You may find that you are satisfied with your achievements but see that you are not actually attaining the goals that you planned. Other times, you may find that you are dissatisfied with your accomplishments, even though you seem to be hitting all the targets dead center. These types of utility and satisfaction ratings can help you think more deeply about what you want out of your life. Do you really want to become a dancer or have you found that composing music is providing a greater source of satisfaction? Now that you have started your business, do you find that the day-to-day management aspects are a tremendous hassle that leave you drained? How are you interacting with others? Use your satisfaction ratings to re-evaluate your goals and think more carefully about your dreams.

The Ethics of Strive

Picture it: You are at a meeting packed with high-level executives looking for a solution to a company-wide issue. You have carefully prepared a brilliant solution that will solve the problem and launch the company into a new area of growth. You have spent a lot of time on this idea, and it is going to not only help the business, but will catapult you into that coveted corner office. Just before you get a chance to present, however, one of your colleagues suddenly commandeers the meeting—with your ideas. Not only are your ideas being pitched by your coworker, but you notice that some of the slides look very similar to those you have created. You've been robbed—of your ideas, your success, and your faith in mankind. Your coworker gets the position you always wanted and is now enjoying the success that you actually deserve.

Sound far-fetched? This kind of scenario plays out in various ways across the globe as people try to grab what they think is "success." It doesn't have to be as blatant as the preceding scenario; it could be so subtle that is almost unrecognized. But it is still there. The desire to achieve "success," money, or power overcomes our responsibility to do what is right. Coworkers may steal the work or ideas of others, or even attempt to slander their colleagues' integrity. Employers may engage in "wage theft," a range of actions that include forcing workers to work before clocking in or work after clocking out, paying less than minimum wage, or purposely misclassifying workers to avoid increased costs. It is not only in the workplace where people behave unethically to achieve success. A spouse might be completely throwing themselves into (very worthy) volunteer work while avoiding the responsibilities he or she has to his or her own family. Younger people may pour themselves into their important collegiate studies while completely neglecting their aging parents. Senior citizens may be spending more time improving their tennis swing than pushing their grandchildren on swings.

While I am not a doctor, I do believe in applying the Hippocratic oath to Strive: Do no harm—especially not to yourself. There are many people who have achieved some kind of "success," but they have hurt the people who matter most or have made the world a darker place by doing whatever they can to achieve their dreams. Can you really say they are successes when they leave a path of destruction in their wake? You cannot live without suffering and causing suffering, but you should choose a path that involves your success that benefits you and those around you. How you choose to strive will have an enormous impact on your world and your enjoyment of your success.

Are you willing to do anything to obtain your goal? Henry VIII (1491–1547) certainly seemed to be willing to destroy anything that got in the way of his dream. He was obsessed with obtaining a male heir to the throne. Instead of considering a different approach to finding an heir, Henry chose to besmirch the reputation of his first wife, Catherine of Aragon (who was, incidentally, originally betrothed to his brother) and locked her away in dreary Kimbolton Castle for the rest of her life. (The climate was exceedingly damaging to her health, and she passed away after only living there for three years.) Henry then rampaged through another five marriages, was willing to execute the innocent in his pursuit of an heir, and caused havoc in his country through his poor behavior (he basically made himself an absolute ruler and head of the church) and lack of financial prowess.

"Success at any cost" could have been the motto of Titus Oates (1649–1705), a man whose pursuit of his passions resulted in destruction and death. Oates seemed to always want to be successful without doing much work, and his blatant disregard for others is a shocking testament to a man who would say anything to get what he wanted. He attended college, but did not obtain a degree. Instead, he lied about having one to get a license to preach, which eventually led to him being ordained as an Anglican priest. He falsely accused a local schoolmaster of a crime because he wanted the man's position. The accusation was eventually proven to be false, and Oates left town and made his way to London, where he became a chaplain on a ship. After losing his position on the ship (and almost his life), he managed to make his way into the Duke of Norfolk's household as a preacher. Oates then realized there was another opportunity in the Catholic Church, so he was admitted to the church and joined the Jesuits. Oates claimed to have a doctorate in Divinity (he didn't). He was eventually removed from the Catholic Church and returned to England, where he pretended to have joined the Catholics in order to spy on them. It was then that Oates contemplated his great ruse—a Jesuit plot ("The Popish Plot") to overthrow the king, Charles II. The entire plot was fabricated by Oates in order to hurt those who disagreed with him and attain wealth and position. The worst thing about Oates's plot was that he was believed—he made over 80 accusations that resulted in arrests. More than 30 people were executed based on his malicious fairy tale. Oates temporarily achieved what he wanted, but eventually was discovered. Not only was Oates imprisoned, but he was also ordered to be whipped five days out of every year. (Incidentally, he was eventually released from prison, but never attained the wealth or fame he desired.)

Striving is not about success at any cost. It is about achieving your dreams, becoming a better person than you are today, and making the world a better place.

Striving, for Life

This guide has profiled numerous people, providing insights into their lives and success (or lack thereof). Although learning from the lives of others is extremely useful, it can sometimes be difficult to pinpoint where we should start in our own lives. Some of the people mentioned here lived so differently that we cannot even imagine how to approach success in the same way (think of Elizabeth I or Alexander Hamilton). I included a short list of ideas in Chapters 6 and 7 that was meant to spur you on to develop some of your own thoughts about how to strive. Here, I would like to take an in-depth look at some of these challenges. Of course, we all want to achieve a modicum of success in our professional lives, but there are a few broad areas where you can develop goals and enjoy a fuller, more successful life.

Building Relationships

How many Twitter followers do you have? How many people are you connected to on media sites like Facebook, LinkedIn, or Instagram? Maybe that number is in the hundreds, thousands, or even hundred thousands. Now, I want you to think of the actual number of people you are connected to who know about your most recent failure, helped you handle a nagging issue, and have recently spoken to about a serious problem that is important to you.

I bet that the number you have come up with is quite small—maybe even one or two. It might even be none. A study performed at Duke University found that many Americans only have two true friends, and that this number is actually lower than it was about 25 years ago (people used to have three friends). That's because Twitter followers or Facebook friends are not in a real relationship with you. Social media can be useful for helping to begin to build connections, but should not be the only way you interact with others. (Incidentally, looking at social media sites may cause you to feel depressed, since we all tend to compare our lives to others. Since people only post the best parts of their lives online, it is easy to become discouraged with your own.)

Relationships are frequently one of the most difficult and challenging aspects of our lives, yet we live completely enveloped in them. Positive relationships can support our ultimate success, not only in regard to reaching our goals, but also in helping out the people around us. Building or rebuilding a relationship takes courage, perseverance, and humility, but there are few challenges that are so satisfying or have such a strong life impact. The challenge we must overcome in building relationships is deeply personal; we must overcome our natural tendencies toward selfishness and pride. Reaching out to others means exposing our inner selves and trusting that we will not be hurt.

There are, of course, some relationships that simply cannot be created or repaired, no matter how hard you try. For example, abandoning an abusive relationship is vital to your health and success. You should never need to worry about your physical, emotional, or mental well-being in any relationship. If you do, you need to leave the relationship. With that being said, there are plenty of relationships where we may be at fault or have not done our best. Relationships require work from both people; they also require sincerity and humility to operate correctly. Taking the first step to mend a broken relationship is a real challenge that can help you grow. Yes, it is very difficult to admit there is a problem, and it is extremely challenging to reach out to others when we are ashamed or feel slighted. But you owe it to your ultimate success and personal growth to mend broken relationships and begin new ones.

Family Matters

It's not popular, I know.

The last figure I saw about the cost of raising a child was around $233,000, and that was without paying for college. (The good news is that if you have more than three children, that number drops by 24% per child, a savings of about $58,000 per little person.) Modern society makes having children seem so burdensome—the loss of freedom, the tremendous amount of sacrifice involved, and of course, the sheer volume of time spent certainly all seem daunting. However, raising children is incredibly risky and entirely about stepping outside your comfort zone to reach new heights of success.

Children are a tremendous growth engine. They teach us so much about life, love, and relationships that simply cannot be learned in other ways. For example, if you have an argument with a friend, you may choose to never see that person again (much to your regret). However, have that argument with your tween and you suddenly realize that you must both work together to solve this problem (which is very difficult, but results in incredible personal growth for you and your rowdy child). Children make us better—and healthier—people. For example, men with children tend to live longer, healthier lives than those without children. Men who were fathers found themselves taking better care of their health and reducing unhealthy behaviors. Both men and women with children tend to enjoy better mental health at an advanced age. Incidentally, married people with children also tend to be wealthier than others. Children teach us to see the future in new and fresh ways, to love freely, and forgive easily (even ourselves).

As a product of the foster care system, I would like to encourage people to open their hearts and homes to those who are less fortunate. There are an estimated 400,000 children in the foster care system, with about 100,000 needing adoption. There are many children who would love to simply have a family to come home to after school. You never know the kind of impact you will have on a single life. I would be remiss if I did not point out the powerful impact a loving home had on my own life. Other adoptees include writer Edgar Allen Poe, Olympian Simon Biles, iPhone creator Steve Jobs, singer Faith Hill, actor Jamie Foxx, civil rights advocate Jesse Jackson, Amazon owner Jeff Bezos, and actress Marilyn Monroe. There are many other children who have been embraced by open-hearted families who can now enjoy real success in their lives because someone was willing to take the risk.

Becoming a Pillar (of Your Community)

You are probably a very busy person.

But are you too busy to make a real difference with your life?

We are inundated with stories and images of people who do amazing things for others: Teens who raise hundreds of thousands of dollars for the elderly, families who fly around the world to serve those in desperate circumstances, or heroes who put themselves into harm's way to save the lives of those around them. It would be easy to think that you have to perform stunning accomplishments in order to make a difference. But that would be untrue. Although all the accomplishments just mentioned are certainly worthy, they are only snapshots in lives that have been dedicated to others—they are, if you will, the Facebook highlights of ordinary people who are embracing change and risk to make a difference. You may never know that the teen who raised so much money had been volunteering in nursing homes since she was 10. Or that the families who fly around the world have been fostering impoverished children for 15 years. Or that the hero who threw himself on a live grenade for his comrades had been on countless battlefields, quietly supporting his fellow soldiers for a decade.

These people made a difference with their lives because they committed themselves to their communities first. They struggled and embraced challenges to change their own world and that of others. You can strive by taking on more responsibilities at work, home, or in the community. Husbands, do you come home at night, sit down on the couch, and watch TV? Striving could include washing dishes or making dinner when you come home. This would be a part of building the relationship with your wife, and it would also help illustrate to your children and community that men also care for their families in ways that are not connected directly to money. Many communities are desperate for volunteers to help the elderly, stock shelves in at a food pantry, deliver meals to shut-ins, clean up local parks, or read to the blind. Churches, synagogues, mosques, and other communities of worship may need a helping hand with mentoring younger people, serving the poor in the area, straightening up after services, or running fundraisers. Do you have a special skill you could share with your local Boy or Girl Scout troop? Have you considered offering to help others learn how to use computers, balance a checkbook, or make cupcakes? There are many ways to get involved in your local community and start striving for success.

Going Pro

Do you feel like your job is a dead end?

Taking on more challenges at work would definitely involve getting out of your comfort zone. These challenges might include discussing a possible promotion with your supervisor or taking college classes at night after work. Sometimes, though, you may find that although you are making enough money and progressing up the hierarchy, you are not truly satisfied with what you are accomplishing. If so, you may need to stretch yourself to find a new career. Changing careers is more difficult than changing jobs. It involves extra study and meeting new people who can help you on your path. You are never too old to learn something new. Learning new things when you are older can be challenging—but not impossible. The ability of your brain to change and adapt, its plasticity, does not change much over time. This means that your ability to learn is a function of your willpower—if you want to learn a new language when you are 40, you can do it. If you want to change careers later in life, you can learn what you need to do that, too. For example, Anna Mary Robertson (Grandma Moses) did not begin her painting career until she was 78. Momofuku Ando, the inventor of the instant ramen noodles enjoyed by college students everywhere, did not invent them until he was 48. (He invented the Cup of Noodles at age 61.)

Feel like a real challenge? Try starting your own business. In today's unstable economic environment, it seems that starting a business might be the last thing anyone wants to do. A study done by Babson College showed that fewer people are striking out on their own, partly due to the shaky economy. However, the growth that occurs when you begin to take control over your own destiny is powerful. Even if you fail, you will emerge stronger, more competent, and better able to tackle new challenges.

Personal Growth

All striving eventually leads to personal growth. However, you may need to face some personal challenges to achieve real success in your life. There are some people who struggle from birth, but they are still able to succeed. Overcoming a disability is not a simple, straightforward process. We are all familiar with the story of Helen Keller, who could neither see nor hear, but went on to earn her degree and become an author and activist. Baxter Humby's hand was amputated when he was born, yet he has gone on to fashion a career out of his incredible athletic talents, winning the World Super Welterweight Championship and serving as a stunt double in movies like Spiderman 3. Gulf War veteran Arthur Boorman beat obesity by changing his diet and pursuing an extreme form of yoga.

Sometimes, achieving personal growth means leaving behind the old ways of thinking. Relocating or living elsewhere forces you to get away from what you're most familiar with and explore new aspects of life and yourself. Have you ever heard that "a change of scene would do you good"? It might. We can sometimes get stuck in a rut simply because we are living in a certain area that does not promote healthy movement. You may, perhaps, live in a cheap studio apartment downtown because you feel like that is all you can afford—and it is close to your job. But finding a place outside the city with walking paths and trees might actually improve your health and wellness. Instead of just moving from city to suburbs, you may want to challenge yourself by living overseas. Once you live in a foreign country, you are forever changed. People who live overseas for a certain period of time tend to be more open and understanding of others. The rising telecommuting trend has resulted in a workforce that is increasingly mobile; these digital natives are working while traveling all over the world. Their view of the world is constantly being expanded as they engage with new communities, languages, and cultures. If you can telecommute for your work, you may find that travel enhances your perspective and builds your creativity.

There is a final addition to this list, and it is something that I would like everyone to consider. No matter your stage of life, no matter your situation, there is an area of personal growth where you can personally make a difference—now. It involves a close examination of your values and perhaps a little research to inform your opinion.

That's Right—Speak Out

You don't need to speak out at a large gathering to be heard. You can simply do it daily (politely), in the company of friends or colleagues. It is simple, scary, and powerful: Speak out against evil wherever you find it. Things like racism, sexism, ageism, and materialism are constantly bombarding us, whether we see them on TV or hear about them at work. Have you ever found that you were silenced because of the crowd—or the boss? A powerful way to achieve success in your life is to speak out for what is right. You will probably never suffer in the same way as Jimmie Lee Jackson, who was killed protecting his family during a civil rights march in 1965, or persecuted like Ayaan Hirsi Ali, who has been the target of death threats because of her opposition to many evils, but you will experience personal growth—and will make the world around you a better one.

Striving Together

Striving is a personal journey, but it is not something you do alone. Strivers are part of a community. I would like to offer you my best wishes on your journey to success. I am interested in learning about your personal growth and success on your path to achieve your dreams. How are you striving to reach your dreams? What changes have you made in your life to achieve your goals? How are you impacting others? Share your personal story about your journey on my site, https://scottamyx.com.

INDEX